T0277475

Cambridge Elements ☰

Elements in Austrian Economics
edited by
Peter Boettke
George Mason University

THE ORIGINS AND CONSEQUENCES OF PROPERTY RIGHTS

Austrian, Public Choice, and Institutional Economics Perspectives

Colin Harris
St. Olaf College

Meina Cai
University of Connecticut

Ilia Murtazashvili
University of Pittsburgh

Jennifer Brick Murtazashvili
University of Pittsburgh

CAMBRIDGE
UNIVERSITY PRESS

CAMBRIDGE
UNIVERSITY PRESS

University Printing House, Cambridge CB2 8BS, United Kingdom

One Liberty Plaza, 20th Floor, New York, NY 10006, USA

477 Williamstown Road, Port Melbourne, VIC 3207, Australia

314–321, 3rd Floor, Plot 3, Splendor Forum, Jasola District Centre,
New Delhi – 110025, India

79 Anson Road, #06–04/06, Singapore 079906

Cambridge University Press is part of the University of Cambridge.

It furthers the University's mission by disseminating knowledge in the pursuit of
education, learning, and research at the highest international levels of excellence.

www.cambridge.org
Information on this title: www.cambridge.org/9781108969055
DOI: 10.1017/9781108979122

© Colin Harris, Meina Cai, Ilia Murtazashvili, and Jennifer Brick Murtazashvili 2020

First published 2020

A catalogue record for this publication is available from the British Library.

ISBN 978-1-108-96905-5 Paperback
ISSN 2399-651X (online)
ISSN 2514-3867 (print)

The Origins and Consequences of Property Rights

Austrian, Public Choice, and Institutional Economics Perspectives

Elements in Austrian Economics

DOI: 10.1017/9781108979122
First published online: November 2020

Colin Harris
St. Olaf College

Meina Cai
University of Connecticut

Ilia Murtazashvili
University of Pittsburgh

Jennifer Brick Murtazashvili
University of Pittsburgh

Author for correspondence: Ilia Murtazashvili, ilia.murtazashvili@pitt.edu

Abstract: Property rights are the rules governing ownership in society. This Element offers an analytical framework to understand the origins and consequences of property rights. It conceptualizes of the political economy of property rights as a concern with the follow questions: What explains the origins of economic and legal property rights? What are the consequences of different property rights institutions for wealth creation, conservation, and political order? Why do property institutions change? Why do legal reforms relating to property rights such as land redistribution and legal titling improve livelihoods in some contexts but not others? In analyzing property rights, the authors emphasize the complementarity of insights from a diversity of disciplinary perspectives, including Austrian economics, public choice, and institutional economics, including the Bloomington School of institutional analysis and political economy.

Keywords: Austrian economics, public choice, institutional economics, Bloomington School of institutional analysis, property rights, self-governance, anarchy

JEL classifications: B52, B53, D7, K11, O1

ISBNs: 9781108969055 (PB), 9781108979122 (OC)
ISSNs: 2399-651X (online), 2514-3867 (print)

Contents

1. Introduction

1.1 The Renaissance of Institutional Analysis

Douglass North won a Nobel Prize in economics in 1993 for explaining how institutions affect the wealth and poverty of nations. According to North (1990), institutions are the formal and informal rules of the game that liberate and constrain individuals and groups in their attempts to achieve their goals. North's conception of institutions is broad enough to encompass all types of rules, including constitutional and procedural rules, laws and legislative rules, and norms and social conventions (Palagashvili, Piano, and Skarbek 2017). Analysis of these rules provides tremendous insights into economic development, the extent to which societies suffer the tragedy of the commons, and political order and violence (Alston et al. 2018). As Rodrik, Subramanian, and Trebbi (2004) remark, "Institutions rule." Liberal institutions – those that encourage productive specialization, exchange, and peaceful transfer of political power – are especially important in explaining human progress and prosperity (McCloskey 2019).

    The growing consensus in economics and political economy that institutions matter is not so much a revolution as a renaissance of ideas that have been around for centuries.[1] Adam Smith's *The Wealth of Nations*, published in 1776, is best known for showing that mutually self-interested exchange can result in outcomes that are socially beneficial – perhaps the most important idea in all of modern economics. Yet Smith was keenly aware of the importance of institutions in allowing this to occur, as evidenced by one of his more famous quotes: "Little else is requisite to carry a state to the highest degree of opulence from the lowest barbarism, but peace, easy taxes, and a tolerable administration of justice."

    Starting in the middle of the twentieth century, the economics discipline became increasingly formalized through the use of mathematics, often at the expense of Smithian humanomics, which understands economic outcomes as deeply influenced by social and moral institutions (McCloskey 2016; Smith and Wilson 2019).[2] Although formalization has the upside of making explicit and clarifying the assumptions that go into any model, insights that are difficult to put in the language of mathematics often must be excluded. This

---

[1] Millenia, even, if we consider the fourth-century BC philosopher Aristotle's *Politics*, which considered differences in outcomes associated with aristocracy, tyranny, oligarchy, and mob rule, as one of the first works of institutional analysis. There has been a renaissance of institutional analysis of ancient Athens in the spirit of Aristotle (Carugati 2019; Carugati, Ober, and Weingast 2019).

[2] The formalized approach to economic analysis has been called the "Max U" approach given its predilection for solving utility maximization problems using calculus.

approach to economics shifted the analysis from a general inquiry into the nature and causes of the wealth of nations to a mathematized clarification of the assumptions and conditions under which market exchange results in efficient outcomes.

Two of the more famous results from this approach are the first and second welfare theorems, which proved Smith's invisible-hand thesis correct – provided certain conditions are met – after more than a century and a half. But the welfare theorems downplay a key part of Smith's insight and explanation. Specifying the exact number of firms or amount of knowledge needed for the invisible hand to work is not the same as specifying the rules under which beneficial exchange may occur. Economic theory became an "institutionally antiseptic" theory of constrained maximization while largely ignoring a leading determinant of constraints – namely, institutions (Boettke, Coyne, and Leeson 2013).

Change would come – not through an abandonment of the economic approach but from an enrichment of the discipline's understanding of what constitutes constraints. Institutionalists provided real-world examples of how people learn ways to get what they want for themselves and their communities. What had been relegated to the background was once again brought to the foreground. Elinor Ostrom's Nobel Prize in economics in 2009 reflected a recognition that diverse institutions contribute to human prosperity and well-being. Yet long before the recognition of North's and Ostrom's contributions,[3] several traditions revived the focus on rules, especially Austrian economics, public choice, institutional economics, and the Bloomington School of institutional analysis.

Austrian economics has since its inception been concerned with the study of institutions (Boettke 1989). As Foss (1997, emphasis in original) argues, Austrian economists, including Menger, Mises, and Hayek, "emphasized the need to have not only an economics *with* institutions, but also an economics *of* institutions." Two central features of the Austrian approach to institutional analysis came out of the work of these three scholars: (1) Institutions often arise and change through a spontaneous and emergent process; and (2) different institutional arrangements have different effects on the creation of knowledge and dispersion of information. Consider, for example, Menger's (1892, 38) explanation of the origin of money as a "spontaneous outcome, the unpremeditated resultant, of particular, individual efforts of the members of a society" rather than a state-imposed institution mandated by law. Or consider Hayek's

---

[3] Boettke, Coyne, and Newman (2016) include Friedrich Hayek, James Buchanan, Ronald Coase, and Vernon Smith as Nobel laureates who continue the themes of Adam Smith, along with Douglass North and Elinor Ostrom.

(1988) extension of the concept of spontaneous order to explain the emergence of other market institutions such as law, including property law. According to Hayek, it was the emergence of these institutions that made possible the Great Society, in which individuals routinely buy, sell, and exchange without knowing one another.

The other central feature of the Austrian emphasis on institutions relates directly to the institution of property and comes from Ludwig von Mises's analysis of the role of property in rational economic calculation. Mises's (1935) argument is simple: Without private property, there can be no exchange; without exchange, there can be no exchange ratios, or prices; and without prices, we cannot solve the economic question of how to make rational production decisions. From the Austrian perspective, property rights play an essential role in the creation of knowledge of the opportunity cost of resources. Hayek (1945) continued this theme and furthered the argument against centralized planning by highlighting the ability or inability of different institutional arrangements such as the price system to generate, collect, interpret, and use dispersed knowledge to rationally calculate economic activity.

Whereas Austrian economists are primarily concerned with the knowledge-generating properties of institutions, public choice economists highlight the issue of incentives.[4] Public choice economics, spearheaded by James Buchanan and Gordon Tullock, clarifies how political institutions influence the behavior of self-interested political decision makers and has been described as "politics without romance" as it rejects the notion that political decision makers necessarily have incentives to do what is in the interest of society (Buchanan 1984). Public choice economists emphasize the structure and enforcement of political rules, drawing insights from classical economists such as Adam Smith, whose sophisticated constitutional theory recognized the role of political constraints as a foundation for economic development (Weingast 2017). This emphasis and intellectual history are exemplified by Robert Tollison's preface to Brennan and Buchanan's (1985) *The Reason of Rules: Constitutional Political Economy*:

> The notion that rules may substitute for morals has been familiar to economists and philosophers at least since Adam Smith. And, of course, the great intellectual discovery of the eighteenth century was the spontaneous order of the market, the discovery that within an appropriate structure of rules ("laws and institutions" in Adam Smith's phraseology), individuals in following their own interests can further the interests of others. The result is the great network of social coordination – refined and extended to the boundaries of the division of labor – that even after centuries defies the imagination when

---

[4] This claim is, of course, not mutually exclusive. After all, one of the standard assumptions from public finance theory that Buchanan (1949, 1986) famously relaxed is the one of omniscience.

evaluated as a cooperative enterprise. The cooperation of agents in a market, however, requires neither that such agents understand the structure nor that they transcend ordinary precepts of morality in their behavior. What it does require is an appropriate "constitutional context" – a proper structure of rules, along with some arrangements for their enforcement.

In addition to incorporating Smithian insights, Buchanan was also heavily influenced by English political economist Thomas Hobbes. As expressed in *Leviathan*, published in 1651, Hobbes believed that state building is a bargain between citizens and the sovereign in which the sovereign establishes the rule of law in exchange for collecting a tax. Buchanan, like Hobbes, was a contract theorist interested in the origins of the rule of law. However, unlike Hobbes, who believed that a monopoly on coercion results in the emergence of good order and working relations, Buchanan recognized that whether this bargain generates a good order depends on the rules in place. A state requires the right rules to ensure the protection of minority interests, avoid predation, and encourage wealth creation. Such rules are critical to address what Weingast (1995) calls the sovereign's dilemma: Political power always corrupts, and a state strong enough to protect rights is also strong enough to violate them. Accordingly, the challenge public choice economics poses is how to design rules such that self-interested political decision makers have the incentives to do what is in society's interest (Buchanan 1975).

Institutional economics includes a broad range of perspectives but can be separated into the old and new traditions. Compared to the new institutionalists, the old institutionalists put more priority on empirical evidence and historical contingency than theory. The new institutionalists are more committed to deductive theory and use empirics and history to test theoretical propositions (Hodgson 2002). This is not to say the old institutionalists do not have theory; they do, but their theory of change emphasizes the importance of governments' establishment of a legal framework to regulate complex interactions in a modern economy (Deakin et al. 2017; Hodgson 2015a).

Despite these important differences, both perspectives appreciate that wealth creation depends on the institutional matrix of society. They also agree that the extent to which rules encourage and enable individuals to participate in markets is a key question in the analysis of institutions. Institutional economics presents an empirically rich view of property creation and enforcement by emphasizing both the costs and benefits of different institutional arrangements for governing the ownership of resources.

One sub-branch of new institutional economics that played a large role in the renaissance of institutional thought is the Bloomington School of institutional analysis and political economy, which originated with the work of Vincent and

Elinor Ostrom. The Bloomington School focuses on citizenship, public entrepreneurship, and self-governance and shows that a remarkable diversity of institutions contribute to economic development (Aligica 2018). Vincent Ostrom's work focused on the importance of polycentric governance, as did Elinor Ostrom's, with offering profound insight into how such governance institutions work in practice. Their work suggests that good governance is largely a question of the extent to which rules fit the local context, with a key insight of the Bloomington School more generally being that there is no one-size-fits-all institution to generate prosperity; we must think beyond panaceas (E. Ostrom 2007). And, like the Austrian, public choice, and institutional schools, the Bloomington School represents a return to classical political economy, in this case that of James Madison, in its recognition of the importance of institutional design (V. Ostrom 2008).

Although these schools of thought overlap significantly, each offers unique insights that are necessary for understanding the origins and consequences of property rights. Austrian economists present a special focus on the emergence of spontaneous rules with property rights being particularly relevant for generating and dispersing knowledge. The Austrian perspective generates a presumption against the top-down imposition of rules as the central planner lacks the knowledge required to engage in effective reform. Public choice economics highlights the influence that the political system has on the economic order while recognizing that politicians have interests that differ from those of society. Public choice economists point out the incentive issues of poorly aligned rules and investigate the ways in which different institutional arrangements can align or misalign incentives. Institutional economics, including the Bloomington School, recognizes the tremendous diversity of institutions that explain the success or failure of governance arrangements, and it highlights the need for institutions, whether evolved or designed, to reflect the existing constraints.

As noted, the study of institutions has always been a part of economics and political economy, but what was once relegated to the sidelines has reemerged as the central focus, largely because of the perspectives of Austrian economics, public choice, and institutional economics (including the Bloomington School of institutional analysis). In this Element, we synthesize these perspectives to provide a greater understanding of the issues surrounding property rights.

1.2 Why Property Rights Matter

Property rights specify which resources can be owned and by whom and how they can be used. The central distinction between property regimes is whether the rights are held by individuals or by the state. In a private property system, rights to valuable objects are assigned to individuals. Under state ownership, the government is the owner of property. The primary difference between the different forms of property is how they specify who bears the costs and captures the benefits. Private property rights internalize externalities – they align private and social costs – by assigning residual claimancy to the owner such that the owner bears the full cost of resource extraction and captures the full benefits of property use (Alchian and Demsetz 1972; Demsetz 1967).

In this Element, we focus on private property rights because they are associated with wealth creation, effective resource governance, and political stability. The simple correlation between secure private property rights and economic growth that is presented in Figure 1.1 suggests we have good reason to be concerned with private property (the data are from 2018).

Private property rights are also central to resource governance. Hardin (1968) referred to the tendency to overuse resources as the tragedy of the commons. A commons refers to anything used by a group of people, at any scale – anything from a shared workspace to the entire planet (or outer space, for that matter). Though Hardin was writing primarily to argue against the "freedom to breed" and in favor of population control, his illustration of the tragedy that results from "a pasture open to all" refers more generally to the overuse of any resource owned in common. Hardin offered possible solutions to the problem including establishing private property rights to the resource or granting the state complete ownership and restricting public use. All

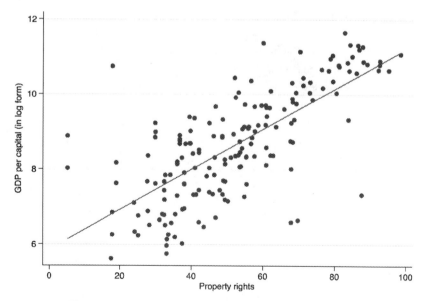

Figure 1.1 Private property rights and economic growth

possible solutions are objectionable, he notes, but "we must choose – or acquiesce in the destruction of the commons."

Insights from the property rights perspective suggest the tragedy of the commons is more specifically a consequence of incomplete property rights (Cole, Epstein, and McGinnis 2014; Frischmann, Marciano, and Ramello 2019). Without clearly defined and enforced property rights, individuals account only for their private costs of resource extraction, not the social costs arising from their use of the resource. The property rights perspective recognizes, as Hardin (1968) did, that some solutions to the problem of open access are better than others as some resources "cannot readily be fenced, and so the tragedy of the commons ... must be prevented by different means" (p. 1245). What determines which property arrangement is better? In large part, it depends on the extent to which a resource is excludable and rivalrous.

Any good can be categorized according to its excludability and rivalry.[5] Excludability refers to the ability to exclude nonpayers from accessing or consuming the resource. Rivalry refers to the extent to which one's use of a good or service precludes others' use of it. Rivalry is generally considered an inherent characteristic of the good, while excludability comes in degrees and is largely determined by the existing technology and capacity to leverage violence for enforcement of property rights.

Private goods are excludable and rival; they are goods and services commonly supplied in markets. Public goods are non-excludable and nonrival so that once they are provided, all can enjoy the good as much as they like without affecting others' ability to do so.[6] Like public goods, club or toll goods are nonrival, but it is less challenging to limit access to them. Examples include toll roads, radio spectrum, and community pools.[7] A common pool resource is non-excludable and rival, with standard examples including fisheries and pastures. Table 1.1 summarizes these four types of goods based on the characteristics of excludability and rivalry.

The resources in question in Hardin's analysis are common pool resources characterized by open access – "a pasture open to all." Because nonpayers

---

[5] The terms "rival," "subtractable," "divisible," and "depletable" are used interchangeably to reflect goods for which there is competition over their use.

[6] Because excludability depends on technology and costs of exclusion, many public goods, such as highways, police, and lighthouses, are provided privately (Candela and Geloso 2018; Clark and Powell 2019).

[7] Buchanan (1965) designates these types of goods as club goods while others refer to them as toll goods. Some club goods are only nonrival to a limit, which suggests an optimal number of members in the club. Past the optimal number of resource users, the good becomes rival. Compare a toll road that could still suffer from problems of congestion if the toll is priced too low to a good like radio spectrum, which (largely) remains nonrival regardless of the number of users, though the spectrum itself is subject to congestion.

Table 1.1 Four types of goods

		Extent of rivalry	
		High	Low
Difficulty of establishing property rights	High	Common pool resource	Public good
	Low	Private good	Club or toll good

Source: Adapted from Ostrom (2010a)

cannot be excluded, individuals have the incentive to only think about their own use, and in their use, they generate externalities. How should this be resolved to encourage conservation of the resource rather than giving in to the tragedy of its overuse? Whether individual ownership, closed-access communal ownership, state ownership with restrictive access, or some other system, the optimal solution depends in part on conditions such as the general cost of creating, defining, and enforcing rights, a cost that depends in part on the existing technological limitations of excluding outsiders from use of the resource and the capacity of the state to act as a neutral third party. In many settings, private ownership is the best means to encourage conservation (Demsetz 1967); in others, co-ownership is more effective than private or state ownership (Anderson and Hill 1983; Ostrom 1990); and in still other instances, state management is appropriate (Bromley 1991). It may even be the case that one property regime is optimal until the technological constraints affecting enforcement costs change (Anderson and Hill 2001). For instance, Anderson and Hill (1975) document how the invention of barbed wire altered the calculus of choice of landownership arrangements governing herding on the Great Plains so that co-ownership became private ownership with the introduction of the new technology.

1.3 Dimensions of Property Rights

Property rights regimes vary along four main dimensions: clarity of allocation, security from trespass, alienability, and credibility of persistence (Eggertsson 1990; Riker and Weimer 1993). Clarity of allocation refers to the extent to which property rights are delineated. Oftentimes, the state helps delineate rights, but in other cases, informal institutions serve such functions. For example, before the Europeans arrived in eastern North America, property rights to land were delineated by stones engraved with the signs of the clan that claimed ownership. According to Anderson and Leonard (2016), this institution served to clearly allocate property rights until the Europeans, who were unfamiliar with (and uncaring about) what the markings meant, arrived. Compare this method of delineation to a modern land registry that is easily searchable online. Of course, such technology wasn't available back then, and Native Americana used what technology they had available, but there is a clear difference between the two property regimes along the dimension of clarity of allocation.

Security from trespass refers to the ability to exclude unauthorized users from the property. As mentioned earlier when discussing excludability, this dimension of property is determined in large part by existing technology and the state's capacity to enforce property rights. Fences, alarm systems, guns, and legal recognition (with the ability to call upon a third-party enforcement agency, such as the police) all affect the ability to prevent trespass.

Alienability refers to the ability to dispose of property as one sees fit, including the ability to sell the property or transfer ownership to someone else. Variation in alienability is mostly determined by legislation rather than physical characteristics. For example, if you own your house, you can rent it out but you cannot legally set it on fire.

Credibility of persistence refers to the expectation that the government will continue to respect rights in the future. Because the state is often relied on to enforce property rights, the sovereign's dilemma of Weingast (1995) obtains: A state strong enough to enforce rights is strong enough to violate them. Political authority can always be used to benefit rulers at the expense of the rest of society (North 1981).

All property regimes vary along these dimensions, not just private property. For example, in some contexts, state property rights are clear and credible, but in others, they are poorly defined, insecure, and inalienable and the commitment of the government to enforcing them is questionable. In the latter cases – weak or failed states – state ownership might not be enforced, in which case informal institutions determine ownership. The inability of governments to enforce state ownership often contributes to the tragedy of the commons, while informal private and community property rights can help to alleviate it.

1.4 Function and Form of Property Rights

The distinction between function and form is critical to understanding the diversity and performance of property institutions. All property regimes serve the same general function of internalizing externalities and governing behavior so that it allows for coordination and encourages investment, economic growth, and stability of expectations. However, property regimes differ in the form they take and consequently in how well they serve their function. Additionally, even property regimes of the same form can differ significantly.

Property regimes are not mutually exclusive and may overlap. Some resources may be privately owned while others are state owned. For example, the government may maintain ownership yet lease out resources for private use. This may include leasing rights to resources such as pasture or minerals (Libecap 2018) or leasing land for other private uses (Ho 2005).

There is also a diversity of manifestations of any of the types of property regime, as illustrated in reform-era China (that is, after 1978). Private property rights were abolished and replaced by state ownership in urban areas and by collective ownership in rural areas under Chairman Mao. One of the economic reforms, the Household Responsibility System (HRS), gave rural households residual claimancy over their output and established land-use rights. However, land remains publicly owned, and the state has authority to expropriate rural land for sale in open markets to fuel economic development and urbanization. This property system has a different form from the private property system that developed in Western Europe and North America, but it still served to encourage investment, as evidenced by China's explosive economic growth (Ho 2017). Households have clearly delineated land rights that are secure from trespass, and they gained limited alienability rights (farmland can be rented out, provided it remains agricultural), yet their rights lack credibility of persistence given the risk of state expropriation. Should the Chinese system be classified as private or state ownership? It's not clear. We prefer to call it selective enforcement because its defining feature is the important differences in definition and enforcement of rights for rural households compared to urban leaseholders.

China's heterodox approach to property may be surprising, but the idea goes back a long way. Léon Walras, in his *Elements of Pure Economics, or a Theory of Social Wealth* (originally published in French in the 1870s), proposed nationalizing land. Walras thought that land could be nationalized and then rented out perpetually, thereby providing people with economic opportunities and providing the state with a reliable source of revenue. He hoped that such a plan would eliminate the need for taxes, under a belief that land's productivity and hence value would continually increase. A key difference from China's regime is that Walras believed that the state would purchase the land at the market price rather than nationalize it. Similar ideas can be found in Henry George's *Progress and Poverty*, published in 1879.

Legal recognition of property and state enforcement of property rights are part of the foundation of all rich capitalist economies, yet an appreciation of the diversity of institutions requires recognizing that state involvement in defining and enforcing property claims can be functional or dysfunctional. Not all states and thus not all property regimes are created equal. Where a state is dysfunctional, informal rights and self-governance often work better than the alternative (Leeson 2007c, 2014a; Leeson and Williamson 2009). Additionally, it does not always make sense, contrary to what Hernando de Soto (2000) suggests, to provide people with legal titles, which are judicial documents specifying ownership. The reason is that, in many instances, the state's entry into land governance can make communities worse off by increasing the authority of political decision makers (Leeson and Harris 2018b). When informal governance is robust and the state is predatory, the state may do well for the poor by simply declining to enforce laws rather than legally recognizing property rights (Holland 2017).

1.5 The Necessity of Political Economy

The fact that the different forms of property regimes are influenced by the functionality of the state, the characteristics of resources, and the existing technological limitations, among other things, highlights the necessity of political economy when thinking about the origins and consequences of property rights. Political economy can be thought of as a discipline concerned with understanding the emergence of institutions and their consequences through investigating the influences of both the economic and political–legal realms. It also embraces the fact that economic and political institutions are often interrelated, or entangled, in complex ways (Conning and Robinson 2007; Wagner 2016).

Our analysis of property is concerned with the origins and consequences of these institutions. As Riker and Weimer (1995) and Weimer (1997) observe, even if we can understand the consequences of property rights, including their effect on wealth creation, their origins are a separate question. Finally, it is necessary to consider why property rights change, whether as a reflection of efficiency considerations or as a reflection of their main alternative, which is redistribution of wealth.

1.6 Outline

Section 2 considers the emergence of economic and legal rights. Section 3 analyzes the consequences of property rights institutions for wealth creation, resource conservation, and political conflict and violence. In Section 4, we contrast the efficiency view of institutional change with a distributional perspective that focuses on the constraints on the emergence of wealth-maximizing property institutions. Section 5 considers two areas of land reform – land redistribution and land titling – and the challenges arising from land grabbing and return of refugees. Section 6 concludes the Element.

2. The Origins of Property Rights

2.1 Economic Property Rights

Yoram Barzel (1997: 3–4) distinguishes between two related types of property rights: economic property rights and legal property rights. Drawing on Alchian (1965) and Cheung (1969), Barzel considers economic rights to be "the individual's ability, in expected terms, to consume the good (or the services of the asset)." With economic property rights, individuals do not have complete control over the resource, whether because of theft or restrictions on its use and exchange. This conception of a property right is distinguished from what Barzel calls legal property rights, which are "rights recognized and enforced, in part, by the government." Legal rights may coincide with and enhance economic rights, but legal rights are not necessary to enjoy economic rights. It is also important to note that neither economic nor legal property rights are absolute, and they can change considerably and often. The two distinct types of property rights may also have different origins.

Because economic property rights often serve economic functions but do not depend on recognition from the state, their historical origin often corresponds to social orders that developed alongside or even outside the context of the state. In the first volume of *Law, Legislation and Liberty* (1973, chapter 2), Hayek distinguishes directed social order (what he calls taxis) from self-generating social order (cosmos).[8] Taxis is made order, while cosmos is spontaneous, or grown, order. Spontaneous order results from deliberative action but not a unified plan. Ellickson (1991: 184) captures the wonder of spontaneous order: "The stuff of a civilization consists largely of its substantive norms. These norms identify the everyday behaviors that call for the informal administration of rewards and punishments. In a well-functioning civilization, these informal rules – which have no identifiable author, no apparent date of origin, no certainty of attention from historians – are among the most magnificent of cultural achievements."

Ellickson emphasizes order without explicit design or formal enforcement, but, as Boettke and Coyne (2005) argue, one may consider a broader conception of cosmos to include institutions of self-governance that provide a forum for deliberation and an organization for enforcement. Under this broader conception, Elinor Ostrom's studies of the commons can be thought of as analyses of spontaneous order even though the governance structures she investigates include explicitly designed mechanisms for deliberation and the enforcement of rules.[9]

---

[8] *Taxis* and *cosmos* are the ancient Greek words for arrangement and world (or order), respectively.

[9] McGinnis (2005) argues that in contrast to Boettke and Coyne's (2005) broader consideration of spontaneous orders, the studies of Elinor and Vincent Ostrom have little to do with spontaneous order.

The same holds for institutions such as prison gangs, which are also unplanned but are able to enforce rules and deliberate about them. What matters for the conception of economic property rights is not so much that they may have emerged spontaneously as that they are defined and enforced without relying on the state; that is, they are created and held by individuals. Thus, it is useful to think of economic rights as resulting from both orders without explicit design or organized enforcement and those that emerged spontaneously and are enforced by organizations whose authority does not reside primarily in a government. We refer to economic rights that originated outside the state as spontaneously emergent because they did not develop by decree as part of a unified plan.

2.1.1 The Spontaneous Emergence of Private Property Rights in Europe and North America

The institution of private property did not originally come about as a directed order from the state. It arose spontaneously and was later codified. An important example of this is the enclosure movement establishing private property in Europe as feudalism declined. Feudalism emerged in France during the Norman rule starting around AD 900. Under feudalism, the sovereign owned all property. The glue holding the feudal arrangement together was an oath of fealty to a lord by those who served and defended his realm. The feudal economic system granted rights to use land to serfs and ultimate decision-making authority to the lords. Lords eventually began to allow and even finance the enclosure of additional lands that were previously considered wastelands, land that they no longer found cost-effective to maintain under their direct control (North and Thomas 1973, 36–38). Monarchs would still claim legal rights to the realm during the enclosure movement (Salter 2015); however, these spontaneous economic property rights institutions constituted the origin of what would eventually become alienable, secure, and legally recognized private property rights.

Not all spontaneous property rights are maintained over the long run and codified as legal rights. In the western parts of North America, nomadic American Indian tribes marked their arrows to establish private ownership over buffalo to reward the most proficient hunters (Benson 2006), much like the rule "Iron holds the whale" that emerged among whalers on the high seas in the eighteenth century or the rule of marking one's claim to driftwood in England by placing two stones on a piece of wood for collection later (Sugden 1989).[10] However, as European expansion continued, Native Americans lost their land. The settlers, with support of the European monarchs

---

[10] Deal (2016, 58–81) provides a history of the property system of "Iron holds the whale."

who laid legal claim to the New World, began to implement the property rights institutions that they knew in Europe. European sovereigns gave rights of land disposal to powerful individuals, who then encouraged settlement. Sometimes settlers received land for free to provide a buffer between the frontier and the nascent towns.[11]

Sometimes property rights that originate from a legal declaration have little bearing on economic rights to a resource as the state may have limited ability to police access to the resource. This is largely the case for the origins of property rights on the American frontier after the Revolutionary War. After the Americans defeated the British and agreed on a constitution, the federal government acquired vast amounts of land through war and treaty. Starting in 1789 and continuing until 1853, the American government acquired 1.2 billion acres of land. These public lands were auctioned off following the guidelines passed in the Land Ordinance of 1785 and the Northwest Ordinance of 1787. These ordinances provided a framework for establishing in the frontier regions the private property rights that served as the basis for subsequent economic growth (North and Rutten 1987). The formal system to allocate land was called the Rectangular Survey System (RSS). The RSS was much simpler than the British metes-and-bounds system: The RSS allocated land in large rectangular sections, whereas the British system demarcated land based on geography. As a result, the RSS reduced the costs of allocating and reallocating property rights to achieve economies of scale (Libecap and Lueck 2011).

Although the RSS worked well to allocate legal claims to the land, the state was mostly absent on the frontier and could not guarantee enforcement. Instead, people chose to occupy land prospectively, claiming economic property rights through first possession. In some areas, land rights were established by planting crops, a method of establishing boundaries familiar to both European colonists and Native Americans through what are referred to as corn or tomahawk rights. These economic rights were not enforced by third parties, but rather by the individuals themselves.

Although personal enforcement of property rights always occurs even within a well-established legal property system, it was not the only way that settlers established and enforced economic rights in the absence of the state. Because of scale economies in enforcement, spontaneously developed property rights often originate with the efforts of organizations. One prominent example is the claims clubs that developed to secure land holdings on the frontier. The violence of the Revolutionary War proved costly for the Americans, the British, and the

---

[11] Such systems were called "head rights." The homestead policies that started in the 1860s and continued until the early twentieth century were a more recent version of the colonial policy of free land.

American Indians, among whom different groups were aligned with each side and with American loyalists (Hoock 2017). Though not exactly defeated, the British no longer wished to continue a complex military engagement with the Americans soon after they started the war for independence. Even before the British conceded, individuals had already begun to enclose the frontier. In Pennsylvania, settlers established an association that they called the Fair Play System. The constitution of this club (which they wrote down) included property rules, a forum for deliberation, and a simple system of adjudication (usually, a three-person board). This club was not legally authorized to claim land, as the new American government was still negotiating with Indian tribes, but they were nonetheless effective in establishing economic rights on disputed lands.[12]

Additional claims clubs formed in new territory as the frontier expanded. Groups of settlers formed clubs to secure property rights in the Midwestern states of Iowa, Wisconsin, Illinois, and Michigan in the 1840s and 1850s and in the Great Plains states, including Kansas and Nebraska, in the 1850s. The clubs all had similar constitutions that began with a preamble that declared "antisocial" anyone who bid against a member of the club. The clubs used violence to ensure that people went along with their demands and respected their members' claims.

Similar groups were formed by miners who were able to establish economic property rights despite weak legal enforcement. Umbeck (1977, 1981) argues that California during the time of the Gold Rush was an institutional vacuum. Norms emerged on the gold fields that gave rights to the first miner to lay claim to a valuable deposit. Miners had no legal rights to the lodes, yet their rights were self-enforcing because of the equality of fighting skill among miners, most of whom were known to carry guns.[13] Within a year of the discovery of gold in 1848, the miners organized into six hundred mining districts in California, each including hundreds of miners. In a first-person account of these clubs, Shinn (1884) aptly described them as frontier governments: Although they were technically not governments because they did not have the force of law, they did enforce rules governing ownership, deliberation, and adjudication through mining courts; they were the miners' version of the land claim clubs.

Individuals with private property rights may realize that it is in their interest to share access to certain resources. Unlike farmers or miners, who wanted private property rights, ranchers on the American frontier wanted private

---

[12] Murtazashvili (2013) discusses the emergence of these clubs and their relationship to simpler personal-enforcement property systems.

[13] A robust theoretical literature considers how fighting skill can lead to the emergence of property rights through a process of conflict (see Skaperdas 1992), but it generally agrees that such a process is wealth destroying (Hafer 2006).

property rights to their cattle but had an interest in sharing access to the vast plains where they grazed their cattle. The federal government, which owned most of the land they used for grazing, did not make this easy for them. When Congress enacted policies to provide for landownership in the Far West, it typically prioritized agricultural land use, which was not always appropriate given that not enough rain in the region made farming a much riskier endeavor.

Ranchers were largely on their own, but it did not prevent the emergence of the open-range cattle industry by the 1860s. Anderson and Hill's (2004) exceptional study of property rights in the American West finds that ranchers cooperated to address their collective-action dilemmas. Rather than distrust one another, ranchers generally did business; ranchers generally trusted each other and did business with a handshake. This system of governance secured rights to cattle and created an important regulated common property regime. The reliance on norms for governance remained important in the region and industry for more than a century, as Ellickson's (1991) ethnographic study of cattle ranchers in Shasta County, California, shows. By interviewing ranchers in the 1980s, Ellickson found that they still used extralegal norms to govern cattle, including those calling for informal penalties for violating the rules. The community understood the rules, which allowed them to regulate their business without the state.[14] Importantly, property was mostly private: Ranchers owned their cattle and their ranches, and they certainly made efforts to keep track of whether rustlers were using the range. The regulation of entry is best thought of as a private right exercised by a group, though this right was enforced exclusively by the ranchers, not by government.

Umbeck's (1977) and Anderson and Hill's (2004) histories of the frontier show that order is possible without the state, though they have been criticized for overstating the security of the informal property rights and downplaying the presence of the state on the frontier. Hadfield (2016, 2017) contends that the spontaneous-order norms Umbeck finds in the gold mines were not law because they could not change through a deliberative process and there was no third-party enforcement. Additionally, Clay and Wright (2005) suggest the property system in the mining camps was so weak that anyone who did not continually occupy land could see their land reallocated through claim jumping, which referred to the norm that if any miner was not physically present on their mine for a few days, it could be claimed by someone else. Indeed, the mining camp rules often stated that anyone could claim land through claim jumping, which meant that miners had to generally be physically present to keep their property

---

[14] Several decades earlier, Stuart Macaulay (1963) showed that most business contracts are enforced not by recourse to the law but through relations of trust. The economics literature on reputational contracting (for example, Mailath and Samuelson 2006) provides a theoretical justification for such behavior based on the logic of repeated games.

right. Clay (1999) shows that Congress made good-faith efforts to address property insecurity and to sort out competing claims as early as 1851, including by establishing courts to adjudicate claims between private property owners and squatters. One could also consider Hodgson's (2015b) broader critique of the distinction between economic and legal property rights, in which he suggests that an economic property right does not constitute property or a right but instead only denotes possession, which alone is insufficient for the type of analysis property rights economists wish to do.

These criticisms are significant but not defeating. Instead of seeing them as fatal, we can consider the historical successes and failures in order to highlight the characteristics required for successfully implementing economic property rights:

- **The size of communities.** When communities are small, individuals are more likely to understand the norms and resolve disputes without resorting to conflict (Alston, Libecap, and Mueller 1999).
- **Equality of fighting skill.** When some individuals in a community are more powerful than others, they are more likely to attempt to secure property rights by force (Leeson 2007a; Umbeck 1977).
- **Shared culture.** Shared culture, shared language, shared experience with property rights, and shared respect for private property contribute to the emergence of economic rights and subsequently enhance the security of legal property rights (Williamson and Kerekes 2011).
- **Presence of deliberative institutions.** In the absence of rules for deliberating about the property rules, property institutions are less likely to function as legal institutions (Hadfield 2016).
- **Endogenous emergence of judges/lawgivers.** The emergence of private-order judges can reduce prospects for fighting over ownership, provided all can coordinate on a judge (Myerson 2004).

Returning to the example of the clubs that governed interactions among farmers, miners, and ranchers, each provided an apparatus to change the rules and a system to adjudicate disputes. In this regard, they were not like the first-possession norms in which people just followed the rules, with no mechanism to deliberate about them or enforce them. Instead, these self-governing organizations provided a substitute for formal law and provided economic rights that were at times at odds with legal declarations.

2.1.2 Private Property Rights in Criminal Organizations

Many of the organizations involved in establishing property rights on the frontier were hierarchically structured, employed violence for enforcement of their claims, engaged in collusion, and enforced rights that ran counter to legally declared claims of ownership. Thus, it should come as no surprise that the logic of emergence in property rights in criminal organizations is similar to what occurred on the American frontier.

The social–capital literature suggests criminal organizations result in economic underdevelopment because they tend to contribute to amoral familism rather than trust of strangers (Putnam, Leonardi, and Nanetti 1994).[15] Nonetheless, criminal organizations often provide services that are normally associated with government, such as property protection and contract enforcement, in exchange for extracting revenue. In fact, the neoclassical theory of the state as conceptualized by North (1981) views the state as something of a mafia providing protection in exchange for extracting revenue. North and Thomas (1973: 87) describe the state as follows: "Born in expanding warfare, created by intrigue and treachery, the crowned heads appeared to have more the characteristics of Mafia bosses than the characteristics of kings envisioned a century later by John Locke."

Olson's (1993) theory of the origins of property rights provides insight into why a criminal organization or a state might establish economic institutions that encourage wealth creation. Olson's theory begins by assuming that bandits roam the countryside, searching for opportunities for plunder. These roving bandits are predators, extracting what they can from their victims before moving on to the next ones. Eventually, these roving bandits settle down and establish a monopoly on coercion over a territory. The monopoly on coercion is what creates the incentives for the monopolist to respect property rights: The monopolist is a residual claimant over production in its territory and thus has incentives to encourage wealth creation to maximize revenue collection through taxation.

Criminal organizations that are local monopolists forgo short-run predation because they can claim some of the long-run profit in the areas they control (Leeson and Rogers 2012). However, they also have incentives to actively oppose the expansion of economic activities beyond areas they can control, such as exchange with outside groups, which can explain the tendency for scholars to associate organized crime with long-run underdevelopment (Wintrobe 2018). The standard way to interpret the social costs of criminal organization is to consider them as sources of social costs compared to those

---

[15] Social capital refers to features of social organizations, including trust, networks, and informal and formal institutions, that influence the ability of individuals to solve collective-action problems (Putnam 1993). Bonding capital ties together similar individuals; bridging social capital ties together dissimilar individuals (Granovetter 1977). Linking social capital considers the extent to which individuals have trust in institutions (Tyler 2006).

engendered by states. Yet this interpretation falls prey to what Demsetz (1969) calls the nirvana fallacy.

The nirvana fallacy appears when one compares a real-world institution to an ideal one. However, the relevant analysis for considering the success or failure of a mafia or a claims club is to compare it to the state as it exists, not an idealized conception of a state that abides by a perfect rule of law. If the state is corrupt or absent, a criminal organization may be more reliable as a property-protection organization than the state. Indeed, the unification of the Italian state historically undermined property protection because the process involved a dismantling of constraints on political decision makers (Boettke and Candela 2020). In that context, it is possible that mafias are an improvement. Similarly, regardless of whether a claims club is any different from a criminal organization, the claims clubs may have been the best available option for establishing property rights on the frontier, which the state could not reach.

In plenty of other cases, extralegal organizations may also be the best available for enforcing property claims and providing governance. To understand this, a good place to start is Leeson's (2011) analysis of pirate organizations, one of the most sophisticated and successful types of criminal organization the world has known. Pirates had to establish institutions to prevent internal predation, minimize crew conflict, and maximize profit. To do so, they developed checks and balances that allowed crews to police their captains and write democratic constitutions for their members (Leeson 2007b). They also figured out ways to increase their profits, such as by flying the Jolly Roger (the skull and crossbones flag that signified a pirate ship about to attack), which signaled a reputation for violence that enabled them to establish property rights over assets – other ships and treasure – without much of a fight (Leeson 2010a).

The work of Skarbek (2011, 2014) on prison gangs in the United States provides an additional example of how criminal organizations overcome social dilemmas. Like pirate organizations, prison gangs are successful organizations: They preside over prison economies and keep their associated criminal enterprise going when their members are behind bars. And, similar to Leeson's exploration of pirate organization, Skarbek's work finds that prisoners participate in collective decision making and contribute to the provision of public goods even when the formal rules governing prisons are poorly suited to such cooperation. Skarbek (2020) extends these ideas to prison gangs around the world and finds that prisoners learn ways to organize their affairs that enable them to provide goods and services that most communities need: property rights, currencies (so that they can trade), and procedures for mutual protection and dispute resolution that eliminate the need for continuous fighting.

In another fascinating work on criminal order, Shortland (2019) explains how criminal organizations make a business of ransoming. Criminal organizations that kidnap people are highly specialized, like any business, and capable of establishing property rights over individuals: The process of capturing and ransoming people requires the ability to expropriate property and hold people hostage. What is remarkable is that these illegal activities are often highly regulated privately and sufficiently sophisticated so that they are often able to persist even when governments make substantial efforts to limit them.

Criminal organizations also benefit from regulations that improve markets and from state building because they are businesses, and so they benefit from stability (Percy and Shortland 2013; Shortland and Varese 2016). They face challenges – for example, they are more likely to attack each other when resources become more scarce (Castillo, Mejía, and Restrepo 2020), which suggests that competition in the kidnapping market could lead to conflict – but, for the most part, criminal enterprises function much like any other enterprise.

2.1.3 Private Property Rights in Customary Organizations

Customary governance is neither state nor criminal governance. Rather, its rules derive from tradition. Customary governance includes informal, traditional, and tribal institutions that govern the behavior of individuals. In many instances, customary organizations are an important source of property rights institutions, yet, unlike claims clubs, they develop to provide governance beyond just enforcing property claims. And unlike a criminal organization, they are not illegal, though state-building rulers often view them as a threat to their authority. We provide two illustrations of property rights originating from customary organizations: Somalia and Afghanistan.

Self-governance in the Somali case must be understood against a background of colonial efforts to simplify complex indigenous property institutions through a centralized legal process in Africa (Lund 2008). Many of those efforts were unsuccessful, and some contributed to conflict. Part of the challenge is that ownership is only one aspect of a property regime, and in many contexts, ownership is fluid (Schlager and Ostrom 1992). With multiple, competing legal systems, people may have ownership claims under one system of law that conflict with claims under another. In Somalia, communities often continue to assert ownership based on customary law, which is a category alongside formal law and Islamic law. Consequently, formal legal recognition may not be appropriate.

Even if legal recognition could improve conditions, formal law has never been a reliable option for most Somalis, and it especially was not after the country descended into civil war in 1991 when northern clans declared an independent republic, resulting in state collapse. Somewhat surprisingly, economic development improved under the anarchy of civil war (Leeson 2007c; Powell, Ford, and Nowrasteh 2008).

The improvement in economic fortunes is not as surprising when we account for clan governance, which in Somali culture is an inherited lineage that determines people's place in society, including which group they are in. Clans are a significant source of governance in Somalia, including governance to provide physical security (Menkhaus 2007). They also serve as a framework to interpret and enforce *xeer*, which is Somali customary law. Xeer has evolved over centuries to govern relations among pastoralists and settled communities, including governance of the commons. Xeer rules specify which members of clans can use land and specify when, in times of need, those outside the clan are allowed access to pasture. Under the customary rules, clan elders resolve disputes over land, enforce law, and provide a forum for deliberation, including interpretation of xeer by a jury of clan elders.

Customary governance structures in Afghanistan developed in a similar context. The Afghan state has generally been unreliable or predatory. Since 2001 the United States has led a massive state-building effort, but after nearly two decades, the state remains very weak, controlling (as of 2019) only half the country. One of the consequences of state weakness is that the legal property regime is very weak (Murtazashvili and Murtazashvili 2015).

Despite formal institutional weakness, self-governance of Afghanistan at the local level remains robust. Afghan customary governance divides authority into community-based deliberative assemblies (*shuras*, which means councils in Arabic, or *jirgas,* which means circles in Pashto); village representatives (maliks, arbabs, wakils, or namayendas); and religious functionaries (mullahs). Shuras are open to participation of all households in a community, although normally only men participate in public deliberations. They are called to discuss matters of collective importance. A malik represents the face of a village to the outside world and functions as a local administrator. Mullahs resolve disputes, especially over those areas, such as inheritance, that are governed in part by Islamic law (Murtazashvili 2016).

Very few Afghans have a legal property right to their land, yet most have a customary deed: a document that is countersigned by a malik and specifies who owns the land or who has access to the commons. Most Afghans own a small amount of land, and nearly all who own land have customary deeds. Customary forums for adjudication, which are used far more often than state courts, accept customary deeds as valid ownership documents (Murtazashvili and Murtazashvili 2016b). In fact, political decision makers are so untrusted that in the nearly two decades since 2001, governmental and donor projects intended to support legal titling have been ineffective, while projects that simply record community deeds have often been effective in improving ownership security (Murtazashvili and Murtazashvili 2016a, 2016c). As Murtazashvili and Murtazashvili (forthcoming) explain, a central lesson of analysis of land governance in fragile states is that land reform depends critically on understanding what works locally and that establishing constraints on the government would likely result in better land governance even if the government does not provide legal titles.

2.1.4 Communal Property Regimes

Our focus has been on the origins of private property rights under anarchy. Of course, Elinor Ostrom's research on property rights contrasts with much of the private property literature. Ostrom showed that in many contexts, property rights are held in common, with rules governing their shared use. As Ostrom (1990: 103) remarks: "It is not possible to reconstruct how earlier users of Swiss alpine meadows, Japanese mountain commons, the Spanish *huertas*, or the Philippine *zanjeras* devised rules that have survived such long periods. We do not know who originated or opposed various proposals, or anything about the process of change itself."

As states provide some recognition of property rights in only half of Ostrom's (1990: 180) cases, it is probably safe to assume that the governance arrangements she investigates originated in an analogous fashion to the examples of the American frontier. One difference is that the US government was strong enough and willing enough to eventually take over definition and enforcement of property rights, although in much of the developing world, states are unwilling or unable to do so. Though Ostrom is often associated with the self-governance literature, it is important to note that one of her central design principles for effective governance is that the state should provide communities with legal autonomy to govern their property as they see fit. Thus, Ostrom's examples of self-governing property arrangements are typically backed by law.

It is also important to keep in mind that Ostromian norms, such as graduated sanctions, can be used to enforce private property norms. Ellickson (1991) studies how ranchers in Shasta County, California, resolve disputes over wayward cattle. The way ranchers dealt with wayward cattle was through social enforcement, such as norms of returning cattle unless there are persistent violators of the norms, in which case castration of bulls might have been used to send a stronger message. These graduated sanctions, which Ostrom found associated with more effective communal management of property, were helpful to ranchers in Shasta County seeking to keep others' cattle from their property.

2.2 Legal Property Rights

Why do we need legal rights? Informal arrangements often work well in smaller groups when people know one another, but as societies increase in complexity, legal rules become necessary. Third-party enforcement can also be useful so that people do not have to stand guard over their possessions and so that enforcement can become specialized – though, as we will see, political power creates a dilemma concerning how that power will be used.

Hayek (1973, 47) recognizes the importance of spontaneous order and the state's role in maintaining the Great Society of impersonal exchange governed by abstract rules:

> Of the organizations existing within the Great Society one which regularly occupies a very special position will be that which we call government. Although it is conceivable that the spontaneous order which we call society may exist without government, if the minimum of rules required for the formation of such an order is observed without an organized apparatus for their enforcement, in most circumstances the organization which we call government becomes indispensable in order to assure that those rules are obeyed.
>
> This particular function of the government is somewhat like that of a maintenance squad of a factory, its object not to produce any particular services or products to be consumed by citizens, but rather to see that the mechanism which regulates the production of those goods and services is kept in working order. The purposes for which this machinery is currently being used will be determined by those who operate its parts and in the last resort by those who buy its products.

In the Hayekian ideal, the formalization of rights involves what we call *redaction* – the assembly of different spontaneously arising property institutions into a coherent legal framework. A successful redaction identifies which institutions work and builds on them in formalizing the institutions. For this to occur, what is necessary is that there is some political mechanism that provides political decision makers with information about what works. The literature on emergence of property rights considers when legal property rights reflect the demands of individuals.

2.2.1 Theories of Emergence of Property Rights

In Demsetz's (1967: 350) theory of property rights, "the emergence of property rights can be understood best by their association with the emergence of new or different beneficial and harmful effects." In other words, new property rights emerge "in response to changes in technology and relative prices." However, critics of this approach (for example, Bromley 2006; Sened 1997) do not believe that it gives due consideration to the interests of political decision makers and instead assumes politicians simply respond to the demands of the contracting parties (Eggertsson 1990). Libecap (1989a) extends Demsetz's theory to the government. Under Libecap's extension, success in establishing property rights depends on the following:

1. **Gains from contracting.** Contracting for property rights is more likely when there is more to gain from establishing property rights. This is the basic consideration of Demsetz's (1967) approach.[16]
2. **Information.** Individuals are more likely to contract when they understand the extent of the common pool losses and when information about the benefits and costs of establishing property rights is readily available to the contracting parties.
3. **Distribution of benefits and costs.** When the gains from contracting are inequitable, contracting is less likely.
4. **Rent seeking.** Small, concentrated interest groups may oppose contracting for property rights when it does not benefit them.
5. **Political parameters.** Politicians and bureaucrats must have an interest in recognizing and enforcing property rights.

Douglass North's theories of institutional change suggest that two additional factors influence the choice of property rights: ideology and history. Denzau and North (1994) maintain that ideology, or mental models, can lead to mistakes in the choice of institutions. Additionally, past choices can constrain the opportunity set of property institutions, an idea referred to as path dependence (North 2005).[17] North's approach suggests the following two factors contribute to the emergence of property rights:

6. **Mental models.** Ideological support for property rights, or the absence of ideological opposition to private property, improves prospects for contracting for property rights.
7. **Path dependence.** Individuals who secure property rights may have self-interested reasons to oppose the extension of rights (because it would devaluate their own property rights (for example, Ferrell 2019) or to support the persistence of inefficient economic institutions (for example, Baland and Robinson 2012).

---

[16] A broad conception of costs and benefits or "technology and relative prices" could encompass the additions Libecap introduces to Demsetz's theory. Under this interpretation, Libecap is more explicit on the types of costs and benefits but does not offer a unique theory. Leeson and Harris's (2018a) discussion of the cooperation theory of institutional change interprets Demsetz in this way. We discuss this further in Section 4.

[17] The role of the past is the subject of the large literature on path dependence (for example, Liebowitz and Margolis 1995).

Any one of these factors can undermine contracting for property rights. For example, when the gains from contracting are small, the transaction costs of establishing property rights may mean that the benefits of establishing property rights do not exceed the costs, and the open-access losses may continue. In such situations, the open-access losses are considered efficient from the perspective of the contracting parties. Additionally, the contracting parties must recognize the net benefits that do arise. When the losses from incomplete property rights are poorly understood and information is unequally distributed, contracting might not occur despite the potential gains from it.

The gains from contracting are determined in part by the bargaining strength of contracting parties. When both sides of a bargain are organized, the transaction costs of contracting may be lower. When one side is disorganized, it may lead to much higher costs of negotiation. Libecap (2005, 2009) uses this theory to explain the delays in transferring land from farmers to fuel urbanization in Los Angeles from the 1940s through the 1960s.

Rent seeking and political parameters are also important. Often, groups benefit from the status quo and may oppose a wealth-enhancing change in institutions if they cannot capture a large enough share of the newly created net benefits. Politicians and bureaucrats also must have an interest in creating private property rights. For example, McChesney's (1990) analysis of property rights on reservations governed by the Bureau of Indian Affairs (BIA) shows that the bureau had incentives to keep Native Americans dependent on the government. They did so by restricting alienability of property and restricting the ability of Native Americans to leave reservations. Bureaucratic mismanagement also contributed to fractionalized property rights, which further undermined productivity on Native American lands (Anderson and Lueck 1992; Carlson 1981).

Beliefs, including ideology, can also lead to the "wrong" choice of property institutions. Alston (2017) conceptualizes beliefs as an aspect of leadership that influences institutional change. Alston et al. (2016) shows that in Brazil, changes in the beliefs of leaders had an important role in influencing economic growth. The divergence between growth in North and South Korea is another example. The same holds for beliefs during collectivization of agriculture. In these contexts, mistakes governed the process of institutional change (Acemoglu 2003).

McCloskey's (2010) analysis of England's rise provides an especially rich account of the way ideas influence economic development. A critical shift was in how English society viewed entrepreneurship. The changes in these beliefs contributed to the making of the modern world.

Finally, culture may affect the security of property rights (North 2005). Culture can be thought of as socially transmitted beliefs and values that serve both as a constraint on individual maximization and as a lens that influences how people see the world (Storr and John 2020). The state might establish legal property rights, but the security of those rights depends in part on whether individuals are willing to accept those rights (Williamson 2009; Williamson and Kerekes 2011). Thus, property is more likely to be secure when one's culture supports private ownership. An individualistic culture, for example, is more likely to support secure property rights (Cai et al. 2020). Once in place, a culture of property rights protection can have important consequences for the path of institutional change. For example, Ely (2007) finds that a culture of constraints on government among European colonists in North America contributed to security of property rights: Colonists believed the Magna Carta applied to them. Rights of ownership and limits on government appear to have been a part of the colonial culture.

Although this logic runs from beliefs and culture to property, the logic may also work in the opposite direction: Property may contribute to a belief in markets. For example, a legal-titling experiment in Argentina found that settlements that improved property rights protection improved support for markets (Di Tella, Galiani, and Schargrodsky 2007). Thus, the experience with securing rights could contribute to a market culture.

Together, these influences can structure the existing property arrangements, which can, in turn, influence the range of possible future alterations to property rights.

2.2.2 The Sovereign's Dilemma and the Credibility of Commitment

One of the most important questions in the literature on legal property rights concerns the incentive of political decision makers to respect property rights once they promise to do so. This is the fundamental political dilemma of any economic system: Any state powerful enough to enforce property rights as a public good can also expropriate those property rights (Riker and Weimer 1993; Weingast 1995). Political decision makers can attempt to make their commitments to respecting property rights more credible by tying their hands with institutions that increase their costs of reneging (Root 1989). Though this of course does not solve the dilemma, it does make reneging less likely.

Many specific types of institutions can facilitate a credible commitment to private property rights. For example, although democracy often constrains political decision makers, it also leaves open the opportunity for a majority-supported expropriation of rights. The credibility literature emphasizes separation of powers and political decentralization, rather than democracy, as critical to the emergence of effective property rights (Diermeier et al. 1997). In this regard, North and Weingast (1989) argue that the Glorious Revolution of 1688, by limiting the prerogative powers of the English monarchy, increased the security of property rights. Other theoretical methods of political decentralization, such as federalism (Weingast 1995), contracting out enforcement to third parties (Hadfield and Weingast 2014; Liu and Weingast 2018), and competition among political organizations (V. Ostrom, Tiebout, and Warren 1961; Tiebout 1956) can also contribute to a state's ability to credibly commit, as other historical instances of political decentralization, such as the emergence of towns and cities (Mokyr 1990; Stasavage 2014), demonstrate. Adam Smith, for example, believed that the emergence of towns provided a political foundation for the emergence of the rule of law and property security as feudalism began to decline in England (Weingast 2017).

The main takeaway from the credible-commitment literature is that although constitutional rules can improve the security of property rights, political decision makers require self-interested reasons to accept these rules. After all, even after raising the cost of reneging, if they benefit more by violating their commitment than by keeping it, nothing stops political decision makers from doing so. According to Calvert (1995), this means that rules preventing expropriation, including at the constitutional level, must be self-enforcing. For constitutions that establish private property rights to be self-enforcing, they must be transparent and in the interests of all relevant contracting parties. For example, Leeson and Suarez (2016) demonstrate the self-enforcing characteristics of the Magna Carta agreements of 1215 and 1225, which provided limited rights to nobles; meanwhile, the US Constitution, by providing a Bill of Rights with a transparent declaration of limits on the state's ability to expropriate property, coordinated individuals' understanding of their rights (Weingast 1997). Rules can be imprecise and not provide enough of a constraint. Kuran (2020) explains how a zakat, a mildly progressive tax, could have provided the basis for limited government in Islam, but the Quran was too imprecise about it to provide a coordinating element for self-enforcement.

Independent judges can also improve property security. Anderson and Parker (2008) use evidence from Native American reservations to illustrate the consequences of credibility of commitment for private property rights. In the United States, tribal judges on reservations are sovereign, which provides for autonomy but also subjects Native Americans to the potential for predation by the tribal government and the federal government. Federal law provides for "lawless" tribes to be moved from tribal- to state-court jurisdiction. Anderson and Parker find that when jurisdiction moves from tribes, with their localized institutions, to state courts, the security of property rights increases.

Political parties can also contribute to credibility. In analyzing China's economic growth, Gehlbach and Keefer (2011) show that the dominance of the
Chinese Communist Party improves the government's ability to commit credibly
to business interests, thereby encouraging investment. This result should be
intuitive: The state has tremendous power to grant and take away privileges. If
businesses can be certain about who will be in control of the government, they
will harbor less fear that their current privileges and favorable policies will be
revoked. Political dominance suggests stability can result in enclaves with economic growth, though these same linkages can result in inequitable opportunities
for property ownership. Stephen Haber, Armando Razo, and Noel Maurer (2003),
for example, find that vertical linkages among powerful groups, politicians, and
bureaucrats in Mexico resulted in unequal distribution and security of property
rights (we discuss this phenomenon more extensively in Section 2.3).

North and Weingast's (1989) study of the Glorious Revolution is
a foundational study of credible commitment and the object of three important
critiques. First, private property rights emerged centuries before the Glorious
Revolution (Hodgson 2017). Second, North and Weingast overemphasize formal
institutions at the expense of cultural institutions that support private property
rights (McCloskey 2010). Third, North and Weingast's explanation places too
much emphasis on big-bang institutional changes rather than the piecemeal
changes in rules, both informal and formal, that together explain economic
performance (Kopsidis and Bromley 2016). Yet, despite these critiques, North
and Weingast present an important insight: Regardless of how or why we get
there, the benefits of legal property rights cannot manifest unless the government
can credibly commit to not expropriating property.

2.3 Selective Enforcement of Property Rights

Law is often thought of as a public good (Cowen 1992). According to the
public-goods view of property law, the government first establishes general
rules governing property ownership and then enforces the rights of owners
equitably. Yet, as discussed earlier, the threat of expropriation can never be
fully eliminated. The ongoing threat of expropriation even within systems in
which the rule of law is thought to prevail calls into question the view that law is
a public good: People can be excluded, and the resources required to enforce
a claim are rival. As Haber, Razo, and Maurer (2003) point out, governments
routinely provide property protection as a private good available only to some.
Property rights are often selectively enforced.

Because governments tend to be predatory, the selective-enforcement view of
property law is a more useful starting point than the public-goods view. The

shift in starting points also draws out the key question. Rather than asking what causes governments to expropriate, we should ask what leads governments to extend property rights protection more equitably, while fully recognizing that the public-goods vision of law is an ideal unlikely to be attained (Cai, Murtazashvili, and Murtazashvili 2020).

In what follows, we consider a selective-enforcement property regime as having any of the following three features: (1) assignment and redefinition of property rights based on political and bureaucratic priorities; (2) restrictions on who can own property (for example, prohibitions of ownership by ethnicity, gender, or race); and (3) weaker enforcement of property rights for certain groups. We consider several examples of selective-enforcement property regimes. We begin with the United States, which is considered to have a robust private property system. In fact, it has always been a selective-enforcement property system.

2.3.1 Selective Enforcement of Property Rights in the United States

The history of strong property rights in the United States includes a long history of private property (which was facilitated by the establishment of the RSS system centuries ago), allocation of property rights to small plots of land to settlers, separation of powers, federalism, constitutional protection of property rights, and political movements, such as the Republican Party with its commitment in the 1850s to "Free Soil and Free Men."[18] These institutional features contributed to the protection of property rights for many white men, but for many other groups in the nineteenth century, the property regime in the United States was one of selective enforcement.

The initial subjugated groups were Native Americans and enslaved Africans. To explain the development of selective enforcement for Native Americans, Anderson and McChesney (1994) apply the raid-or-trade model to the federal government and Indian nations from the late 1700s through the Indian Wars after the Civil War. Their primary explanation for the US choice to raid rather than to continue to trade is the divergence in military might following the Civil War. For much of their history, Indians had a comparative advantage in fighting. From the federal government's perspective, the cost of raiding for resources – of fighting with natives and local militias – was high relative to developing treaties and trading with the indigenous groups for what they needed. However, the Civil War forced the government to develop and maintain a standing army, which, once developed, significantly reduced the cost of using it to raid others. The result was the dominance of the military over Native Americans west of the

---

[18] Foner (1971) considers the Republican Party's commitment to free land.

Mississippi, which completed the development of the reservation system and subjugation of Indians.

Under the reservation system, the sovereign tribal government was unconstrained, which resulted in its own internal problems on many reservations (Cornell and Kalt 1998, 2000). However, predation from the federal government was more of a challenge than from tribal governments. The Dawes Act in 1887 (formally, the Indian Allotment Act) created a system to help allocate land to Indians so that unallocated land could be opened to white settlers (thereby reducing land initially allotted to tribes when reservations were created), but it also made it exceptionally challenging for Indians to secure property rights in fee simple. The underlying problem was the bureaucrats in the BIA, who, with an interest in maintaining their budget and keeping their jobs, had an incentive to keep Indians poor to keep them on the reservation (McChesney 1990). Despite federal treaties promising Native Americans sovereignty on the reservations, the federal government had a free hand to reallocate Native American land for white settlers when the land was considered valuable enough.

A similar story of selective enforcement can be told of enslaved Africans. The first slave ships arrived in 1619. The institution of slavery continued until the South accepted defeat in the Civil War. Weingast (1997) takes the value of slaves to the owners as given and argues that the persistence of slavery depended on the "balance rule."[19] During the nineteenth century, as the frontier expanded, states petitioned to join the union. The land ordinances allowed for self-determination in the territories, including determination of whether to allow slavery. The balance rule was a norm of admitting a free state with each slave state. Weingast argues it preserved slavery by ensuring that the pro-slave Southern states could veto any legislation or constitutional amendment prohibiting slavery. However, the balance rule was no longer a possibility by the 1850s because there were no more slave states in the west, which meant that slavery would eventually be threatened politically as the march of settlement continued. The combination of the value of slaves to slaveowners and the decline of the balance rule gave the South an incentive to secede to preserve the property institution of slavery.

The histories of Native Americans and of black people in the American South prior to the Civil War are among the most egregious examples of selective enforcement of property rights in the United States. Another is the limited rights of women to own property prior to the twentieth century. Lemke (2016)

---

[19] Though slaves were valuable to the owners, the institution of slavery placed a drag on the Southern economy compared to the Northern economy (Sokoloff and Engerman 2000).

explores the extension of the rights of women to own property in the states and explains the gradual change to property laws induced by an increase in political competition. Polycentric governance created incentives for politicians at the state level to compete for women's support. Lemke's analysis illustrates yet another example of selective enforcement in the United States but at the same time highlights that the extension of property rights often depends in part on political institutions.

These examples illustrate that although the United States has a private property system that has encouraged significant economic growth, it has also had a system of selective enforcement for much of its history, ensuring that many were not able to share in the benefits that come from secure property rights.

2.3.2 Property Rights and Economic Growth in Mexican Economic History

Leeson and Williamson (2009) apply the theory of second best to property rights, development, and instability. They recognize that informal property rights are often robust under anarchy and that the alternative to anarchy is predatory government. Accordingly, anarchy may be second best in situations of system-wide political instability.[20] With instability, despots have incentives to behave like roving bandits, not stationary ones, rendering the rule of law impossible to maintain.

Haber, Razo, and Maurer's (2003) theory of selective enforcement of property rights analyzes whose rights are protected by the sorts of predatory governments analyzed by Leeson and Williamson. In Haber, Razo, and Maurer's theory, property rights consist of rights to use, earn income from, and alienate assets. The government's role is to specify and enforce these property rights though they assume that the government may choose to enforce property rights selectively, as a private good rather than a public good. Additionally, they assume that asset holders (1) do not demand equal protection of property rights, (2) make decisions on a continuum of risk assessments, and (3) cannot perfectly monitor the actions of government, which means the government can tinker with property rights on numerous margins. The result of their model is that the government can enforce property selectively in a mafia-style system. Such arrangements, they argue, are self-enforcing if the government is able to receive tax revenue from those who receive selectively enforced rights, asset holders are able to receive the selective enforcement of their rights, and the third parties tasked with policing and enforcing the arrangement are able to share in the creation of rents from the selectively enforced rights.

---

[20] See Lipsey and Lancaster (1956) for a general exploration of the theory of the second best.

Haber, Razo, and Maurer (2003) use their theory to explain economic growth in Mexico between 1876 and 1929. Excluding the civil war from 1914 to 1917, they find evidence of economic growth in sectors characterized by these mafia-like arrangements despite significant periods of political instability throughout Mexico. They conclude that property rights protection varies within unstable countries, meaning instability may affect industries differently. Where there is a significant coalition of asset holders who seek rents from a government strong enough to influence the enforcement of property rights but too weak to be completely despotic, secure rights might be selectively enforced within the industry dominated by the rent-seeking political coalition. Under their model of vertical political integration, the selective enforcement of property rights is a function of where rents are earned and distributed, yet, nonetheless, compared to a completely unstable system, selective enforcement allows for some economic growth as it provides security to some property rights holders. Though Haber, Razo, and Maurer do not explicitly consider the possibility that anarchy is second best, as Leeson and Williamson do, the theory as applied to Mexico provides insight into why otherwise predatory governments provide property rights protection to some groups and in certain sectors.

2.3.3 Marketing Boards and Predatory Property Rights in sub-Saharan Africa

Notwithstanding evidence from Mexican economic history, selective enforcement often characterizes exploitative property regimes in which the government captures most of the resources. For example, Bates's (1981) analysis of agriculture in sub-Saharan Africa emphasizes marketing boards as an explanation for economic underdevelopment. These marketing boards set the prices farmers could receive for their crops, which the government then sold to generate revenue.

Eventually, the predatory marketing scheme destroyed the comparative advantage of many African economies such that countries that were once agriculturally wealthy had to import products as farmers had little incentive to maintain production and remain on their land. Thus, the government's plans to suppress the property rights of rural farmers to satisfy the demands of their urban constituents for cheaper agricultural products and to generate government revenue caused massive starvation and eventually landlessness. A similar story can be told about Kenya's price control on beef, which significantly hindered livestock production and the viability of private ranches yet was maintained to help urban consumers. The result was that the wealth of ranchers was destroyed; bureaucrats and politicians gained when the now-unproductive land was sold (Leeson, Harris, and Myers 2020; Rutten 1992).

Self-governance remains relevant in contexts of selective enforcement. Using evidence from traders in Nigeria, Grossman (2020) shows that participants in markets are often able to develop institutions of self-governance to protect themselves against predation. The need for such self-protection arises from the presence of an inequitable property rights arrangement.

2.3.4 Selective Property Rights in China and India

The pursuit of industrialization in China and India has been accompanied by the use of state power to dispossess and sell land. Formal legal institutions fail to protect the property rights of rural residents; to the contrary, they make property confiscation legal. As a result, land dispossession has benefited the state and the private sector while rural residents have generally been considered as victims.

China has a dual land-tenure system of state-owned urban land and collectively owned rural land. The commodification of land has contributed to the development of fully functioning urban land markets (Rithmire 2015). In contrast, the development of rural land markets has been limited: Rural land rental markets have gradually developed in which rural households can rent out their agricultural land provided that the land remains in agricultural use. Although rural households are granted long-term land-use rights, they are prohibited from selling their land to urban land users.

Instead, agricultural land can only be converted to urban nonagricultural land through expropriation, a process monopolized by the state. Local governments expropriate rural land while paying land-losing households compensation that is administratively determined at below-market prices and then auction off the expropriated land in competitive urban land markets. The price differential arising from distorted land markets generates windfall revenue for the state (Hsing 2010). Inadequate compensation, forced eviction, and land-related corruption have become commonplace, triggering escalating grievances and protests against land expropriation in rural and peri-urban China (Sargeson 2012, 2013). Heurlin (2016) finds that social unrest is higher in markets with high-value real estate because the compensation that villagers receive deviates more drastically from actual land values.

Land laws grant the state the authority to expropriate land for the public interest, the scope of which they do not define, however (Land Administration Law of China, Article 2). This legal ambiguity gives local governments enough flexibility to interpret rules to serve their interest. Figure 2.1 shows the amount of land converted from rural use to urban nonagricultural use and how this land is allocated among various sectors in China. Though the proportion of land dedicated for public infrastructure has been increasing since 2011, a sizable

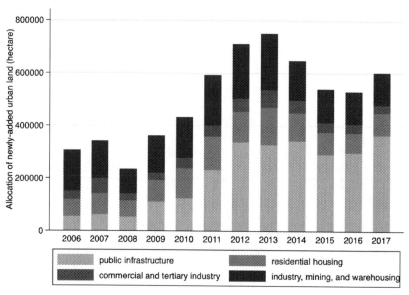

Figure 2.1 Allocation of newly added urban land in China

portion of expropriated land has always been made available for nonpublic purposes to support industrial, commercial, and residential development.

In India local governments have increasingly acted as land brokers that seize farmers' land to benefit private capitalists since the early 1990s. Under the protection of the 2013 Land Acquisition Act, local governments pay land-dispossessed farmers compensation that, as in China, departs significantly from the land's market value. The tremendous discrepancies between compensation prices and market prices have become an important source of protests by farmers against land dispossession. The state-led creation of special economic zones has failed to alleviate the poverty of land-dispossessed farmers because local governments subsidize private corporations with cheap land (thereby resulting in dispossession); however, many of these corporations – for example, those in the high-skilled-service sector – cannot absorb much of the labor of the dispossessed farmers (Levien 2011, 2012). In the end, land dispossession serves narrow beneficiaries while marginalizing farmers, making what Levien (2018) calls "dispossession without development" a defining feature of India's post-liberalization economy.

2.3.5 Property Rights in the Ottoman Empire

Selective enforcement often targets minorities or otherwise powerless groups in favor of protecting those with power and relative strength. Yet this is not always the case. Sometimes even locally powerful groups are subject to expropriation. For example, during the Ottoman Empire, the sultan routinely expropriated tax farmers and administrators instead of peasants. These expropriations (müsadere) allowed the sultan to keep general taxes low, but at the risk that extracting too much from these powerful groups could lead to the collapse of the regime. The risk was worth taking under certain conditions, and the sultan was more prone to target strong elites when overall tax revenue was too low and the empire was at risk of fiscal instability (Arslantaş, Pietri, and Vahabi 2019).

There is much to be gained from comparative analysis of selective-enforcement property regimes. China and Mexico demonstrate the possibility of high growth even with instability and selective enforcement. India is an opposite example. The United States shows that significant economic growth is possible even if property protection is not extended to all groups equally. And as the example of the Ottoman Empire illustrates, even those who are privileged under selective-enforcement regimes may face predation by political decision makers.

2.4 Property Rights and State Building

Property rights also reflect state building. We consider three examples: the settling down of barbarians and the emergence of polycentric governance; the relationship between the increasing scale of collective defense and private property rights; and the political economy of giving away land to create empires.

2.4.1 Barbarian Settlements

Olson's (1993, 2000) stationary-bandit theory of property rights implies that once roving bandits settle and a state emerges, the security of property rights improves. Yet Olson's theory is silent on the process by which roving bandits settle down. Young (2016) fills this gap with historical examples. For example, Young (2018) analyzes barbarian settlements in the Roman Empire and finds that Roman landowners provided barbarians with land allotments. The system provided incentives for barbarian warriors to move from roving confederacies to stationary kingdoms. Because the confederacies still had autonomy in the kingdom, but the kingdom provided overarching rules to govern relations among the different groups represented in each confederacy, the result of this process was the emergence of a polycentric system of governance that gave rise to more robust property rights.

In addition to expanding on Olson, Young (2016, 2018) integrates insights from the credible-commitment approach. The stability of property rights reflected not only political stability (the settling of bandits) but also polycentricity, which is one way to achieve limited government. Despite Olson's claim, the settling of bandits is not always beneficial. Along similar lines, Murtazashvili and Murtazashvili (2016d) argue that the settling of roving bandits may lead to more expropriation of land and create incentives for rulers to use property insecurity to maintain control in the absence of constraints. Further, Boettke and Candela (2020) and Candela (2020) show how state consolidation undermines property rights when governments are unconstrained, using evidence from state formation in Italy to clarify the necessity that political constraints emerge alongside increases in government capacity.

2.4.2 Wealth-Creation Externalities, Property Rights, and Collective Defense

The creation of private property rights can encourage wealth creation but as a result invite plunder. Hendrickson, Salter, and Albrecht (2018) give the example of a primitive society unable to defend itself from external threats. To make predation less appealing for the predator, the society may limit its accumulation of capital and other forms of wealth. Thus, one might expect a state at early stages of development, before it develops a robust system of defense, to introduce policies that actually limit growth and only later be able to finance defense through taxation and borrowing (Thompson 1974). Given that those with wealth would benefit from the development of a collective system to protect their property from predation, we would expect the wealthy to bear most of the initial cost of protection. This perspective suggests that merchants who benefit from property rights protection have incentives to consent to taxation to support the creation of a state with the capacity to provide defense.

Tax policies and regulations are not the only ways to deliberately decrease wealth. Leeson (2014b), for example, considers a similar issue in another, more abrupt form of intentional wealth destruction: human sacrifice. Rather than an irrational practice of pure destruction, human sacrifice can be thought of as an efficient response to the substantial costs of collective defense. In Leeson's theory, publicly sacrificing a person lets would-be predators know there is less available for the taking. The key here is that human capital is valuable, so sacrificing people shows to predatory outsiders that the outsiders have less to gain from conquest. Hence, outsiders have less of an incentive to attack groups that destroy wealth in such a visible fashion. One implication of Leeson's theory is that the destruction of wealth can improve social welfare when there is a chance of predation.[21] Another

---

[21] A similar argument can be found in Scott (2009). Harris and Kaiser (2020), in their exploration of Viking burial practices, identify the related phenomenon of purposeful wealth destruction to avoid internal conflict.

takeaway is that if a society can discover a cheaper way to provide collective defense than the deliberate destruction of resources, wealth creation can be encouraged despite external threats.

2.4.3 State Building by Giving Away Property

Property can also be used to fund state building. According to Murtazashvili (2013), squatters on the US frontier undermined the ability of the federal government to provide public goods by colluding during government land auctions. Allen (1991a, 2019) argues that auctions are not necessarily the best way to allocate land, especially when the costs of allocating land in this manner are substantial. It can make more sense to give land away. In the United States, there was also a benefit from reducing as much as possible the costs of migration to the frontier in the nineteenth century. The homestead law, under which land was given away, reduced the costs of policing the frontier during the Indian Wars as individuals occupied land prospectively to secure the most valuable land. A problem with giving away land is that the reduced prices can lead to dissipation of land values as individuals compete to establish first-in-time claims to land (Anderson and Leonard 2019; Anderson and Hill 1990; Lueck 1995).

2.5 Toward a Theory of the Origins of Property Rights

Although property rights may emerge spontaneously and be enforced privately, they typically are developed by organizations, whether the state or extralegal organizations, because of scale economies in enforcement and defense (North 1990). The literature also suggests that the emergence of successful economic or legal rights typically reflects a similar set of conditions:

- **Monopolies on coercion in a fixed territory.** Control over territory creates incentives for decision makers to respect property institutions and invest in their maintenance, while threats to such monopolies contribute to insecurity of property rights.
- **Governance capacity.** Any property regime depends for its success on the capacity of an organization to administer and enforce property rights.
- **Institutions to acquire information.** Because governments do not necessarily have information about which property institutions are best for the claimants, the presence of institutions that enable political decision makers to acquire information about local conditions and local needs is essential to the creation of effective property rights.

- **Institutional constraints.** Constraints on decision makers are necessary to ensure that those with political power respect the property rights of individuals and communities.
- **Inclusive institutions for collective action and adjudication.** The inclusivity of institutions, or the extent to which they allow individuals and groups access points to political deliberations regarding the definition and enforcing of property rights, is especially important to making provision of property rights less selective.
- **Supportive social institutions.** Social institutions can either enhance or undermine security of property rights.

These conditions exclude many examples of spontaneous property rights, such as those found in Benson (1989a, 1989b), Demsetz (1967), Anderson and Hill (1975, 2004), Ellickson (1991), Leeson (2007b, 2007d, 2009), Kerekes and Williamson (2012), Harris (2018, 2014), Smith, Skarbek, and Wilson (2012), Friedman (1979, 2005), Murtazashvili and Murtazashvili (2015), and Scott (2009). These examples demonstrate the emergence of property rights in a state of anarchy and thus do not meet the condition of being created by an organization with monopolistic control over a fixed territory. And although this literature is open to the critique that such norms and property arrangements do not constitute law (Hodgson 2009, 2015a, 2015b), it is not difficult to conceptualize these nonstate arrangements as generating productive quasi-legal property rights. The rights are quasi-legal because they do not come from the state but have all the requisite feature of a law: They are well understood and enforced, and the rules can change through a deliberative process.

The framework also highlights the role of the state in the emergence of effective property rights, including common property. Elinor Ostrom's research on the commons provides a remarkably rich framework to study governance of the commons that at its core views the sustainability of social–ecological systems as depending on very basic features of political institutions: democracy, separation of powers, administrative capacity, and control over territory. In fact, one of Ostrom's (1990: 90) design principles for ensuring that governance institutions will be long enduring includes the "minimal recognition of rights to organization . . . to devise their own institutions [and] not [be] challenged by external governmental authorities." In this case, the design comes from the users of the resource, and the institutions are their own in the sense that they have the primary role in deliberations about changing those rules. Any complex self-governing property system is, for example, typically unable to defend itself against warlords or commanders in a fragile state, let alone a strong state that does not recognize its right to govern. And whether external authorities respect self-governance is likely to depend on the presence of robust institutions for self-governance, as emphasized in the literature on political polycentrism. It appears useful to integrate Ostrom's perspective more deeply with the literature on the sovereign's dilemma, political constraints, and state capacity.

3. The Consequences of Property Rights

3.1 Property Rights and Wealth Creation

3.1.1 Property Rights and Economic Growth in Economic History

North and Thomas's *The Rise of the Western World* (1973) attempts to explain how England and the Netherlands surpassed France and Spain economically and militarily between 800 and 1500.[22] Their explanation for this reversal of economic fortunes primarily comes down to property rights: Countries that created stronger property rights experienced growth, while those that prioritized expropriation (and regulation) grew more slowly. This explanation, of course, raises the question of why some countries enhanced their property regimes while others worsened theirs.

The starting point in considering England's economic rise is feudalism, which emerged in the ninth century in Norman France. For several centuries, feudalism provided a foundation for security in an anarchic world.[23] The Norman Conquest in 1066 brought feudalism to England, and with it came the centralization of the state under William the Conqueror – a more centralized state than any on the Continent (Bates 2017). The centralized power of the Crown enabled the King's Court to establish jurisdiction over freemen, which contributed to manorial lords' loss of control and eventually their landholdings.[24]

Over the next several centuries, economic property rights began to slowly emerge, and the conditions for the emergence of markets became favorable even though the Crown still claimed legal ownership over the whole realm. But the Black Death reduced the volume of trade and stimulated a trend toward local self-sufficiency because of declining population, war, confiscation, and pillage. A sharp decline in the population decreased the marginal value of land, leading

---

[22] See also Dincecco (2011) and Dincecco and Onorato (2017) on the economic and political explanations for European economic growth. Some important histories of Europe include Bonney (1999) and Brewer (1990). On the political economy of England and France, see Stasavage (2003).

[23] De Long and Schleifer (1993) offer a similar perspective on feudalism.

[24] The presumed relationship here runs from state capacity to development, though Geloso and Salter (forthcoming) argue that state capacity is a result of development: Once wealth is created, greater centralization becomes necessary to protect it. Because centralization occurred through conquest in England, economic development is more plausibly an outcome of state capacity in that case.

to a weakening of property rights. At the same time, fewer people resulted in an increase in the return to labor and an accompanying increase in the bargaining power and wages of workers (Haddock and Kiesling 2002). The increase in bargaining power made it relatively easy to seek rents from the government and to monopolize trade through government favor rather than expanding production and entering new markets.

Sovereigns, who received much of their revenue from taxing the landed elite, confronted a choice: Encourage production by strengthening private property rights or increase the scope of government to generate revenue from tariffs, monopolies, and the expropriation of land. Spain and France chose the latter strategy; England moved in the direction of securing private rights to land.

In Spain, rather than pursuing a strategy of increased agricultural production to fill the fiscal gap, sovereigns relied on revenue from the Mesta, a politically powerful and wealthy group of nomadic herders. The economic power of the Mesta made them politically valuable (as a revenue source) and destroyed the possibility of enclosure because the Mesta, as nomadic herders, opposed the definition and enforcement of property rights for agriculture. Without enclosure, agricultural productivity was severely hampered. France developed a more centralized, tax-heavy state by the fourteenth century to finance wars with England. The expansion of the bureaucracy increased the ability of the Crown to tax peasants, increased the costs of changing the legal system – preventing an enclosure movement – and gave rise to sharecropping, which emerged in response to limited supplies of land and reduced the efficiency of agricultural production. Bureaucratic expansion also limited the mobility of labor and capital, stifling innovation. To compete, businesses demanded subsidies, which further restricted competition.

England's development differed in important ways. It was, as noted, more centralized early on than the major Continental powers. North and Thomas (1973) explain that the state was centralized enough to provide public goods but not so powerful as to dominate individuals who were gradually breaking the bonds of feudalism. Over time, England's de facto federal system enabled the piecemeal development of institutions to encourage wealth creation on a grand scale while providing a political balance. To use Acemoglu and Robinson's (2019) terminology, England was in the narrow corridor of liberty: It struck a propitious balance between state capacity and a robust society capable of generating new ideas and innovations.

The importance of property institutions is also illustrated through comparing the economic histories of Europe and the Middle East. In 1000, the Middle East represented the frontier of institutional and economic development. Mecca was the world's most vibrant trading hub. Yet over the next 500 years, the economic fortunes of the Middle East and Europe diverged: By 1500, Europe had developed the foundation of capitalist institutions that facilitated impersonal exchange in the Great Society, while Middle Eastern countries began to constrain commercial interactions.

Part of Timur Kuran's (2011) explanation for the long process of divergence is religious institutions related to property. According to Kuran, one source for the initial economic advantage in the Middle East was the Islamic institutions that encouraged trade among Muslims. However, over time, other features of Islam, including the rules governing inheritance, constrained economic development. The rules governing inheritance required property to be divided among heirs. With the religious norm of polygamy, this inheritance rule fragmented property holdings. In Europe, in contrast, fewer heirs contributed to larger landholdings. Similarly, compared to Christian countries where firms could be passed on and outlive their owners, this form of inheritance was limited in Islamic countries. Over time, as economic activities expanded, Islamic institutions constrained the ability of Islamic businesspersons to attain scale economies. Wealth declined as a result. One implication of this analysis, as Kuran (2004) explains, is that it does not make sense to think of Islamic economics: There are only economics and the institutions that shape economic incentives.

The protection of legal property rights often depends on politics, as is evident from some of the previous accounts. Accordingly, political constraints can influence economic growth through their effect on the security of property holdings. In European history, rulers who were less constrained could not commit credibly to respecting property and ultimately had less access to credit (Stasavage 2011). Similarly, North, Wallis, and Weingast (2009) suggest that growth depends fundamentally on open-access institutions that provide opportunities to participate in collective action and allow for accessible opportunities for ownership. And, in explaining why some nations fail, Acemoglu and Robinson (2012) emphasize the importance of political institutions for influencing the evolution of economic institutions.

3.1.2 Socialism and Its Discontents

An important difference between capitalist and socialist institutions lies in the structure of property rights (Furubotn and Pejovich 1972). One of the defining features of the Soviet system was state ownership of property, including land and businesses, which contributed to the breakdown of the economy (Boettke 2001; Kornai 1992). In China, Mao Zedong started to expropriate land in the

1930s, and by the 1950s, he established collective ownership of agricultural land. The combination of the abolishment of private property rights and continuous political campaigns (such as the Great Leap Forward and the Cultural Revolution) destroyed wealth (Dikötter 2010). More recent examples of socialist institutions include those in North Korea, Cuba, and Venezuela. In Zimbabwe, Robert Mugabe's regime established a socialist landholding system with massive expropriation of land.

We can consider the Korean peninsula as a natural experiment to test the impact of socialist institutions on economic performance because North and South Korea shared the same culture and history prior to the Korean War. The most important difference since then has been their economic institutions. South Korea established capitalist property rights and markets, while North Korea chose socialist institutions (Acemoglu, Johnson, and Robinson 2005). North Korea initially had a better foundation for developing its economy than did South Korea because industry and mining were concentrated in the northern areas; the southern areas were overwhelmingly agricultural during colonial rule (Seth 2019). Figure 3.1 shows the increasing divergence in gross domestic product (GDP) per capita in the two countries. While South Korea transformed from one of the world's poorest countries into one of its wealthiest, North Korea has suffered from chronic food shortages, including during the famine of the 1990s.

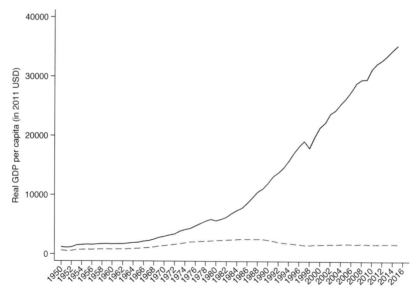

Figure 3.1 GDP per capita in North and South Korea

Capitalism has expanded over time, leading to increasing economic well-being on several dimensions. The Fraser Institute creates the Economic Freedom Index, which measures the extent of capitalism across countries and over time, ranging from zero (completely unfree) to ten (completely free). Figure 3.2 plots the average level of economic freedom in the world since 1980 and demonstrates that capitalism extended rapidly until around 2005 and flattened after that.[25]

Leeson (2010b) shows that capitalism is associated with beneficial outcomes. Using data from 1980 to 2005, he shows that countries that became more capitalist became wealthier, healthier, more educated, and politically freer. The opposite holds true for countries that became significantly less capitalist over this period: They experienced stagnant growth, shortening life spans, smaller gains in education, and a plunge in democracy. Figure 3.3 updates Leeson's study with newer data.[26] It suggests that the beneficial outcomes associated with capitalism still hold when we extend the time span to cover almost four decades. Only one country, Venezuela, became significantly less capitalist over the same period, as opposed to five countries (Myanmar, Rwanda, Ukraine, Venezuela, and Zimbabwe) during the time frame Leeson examined.

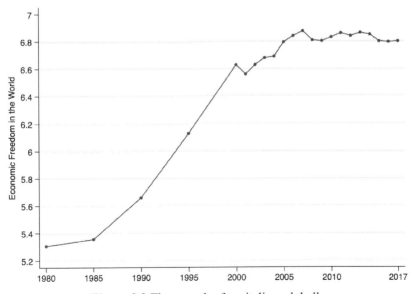

Figure 3.2 The growth of capitalism globally

---

[25] Figure 3.2 is adapted from Leeson (2010b), which depicts the growth of capitalism from 1980 to 2005.

[26] Following Leeson (2010b), countries that became more capitalist are defined by a positive economic-freedom-score change from the first nonmissing value in the range 1980 to 2017.

(a)

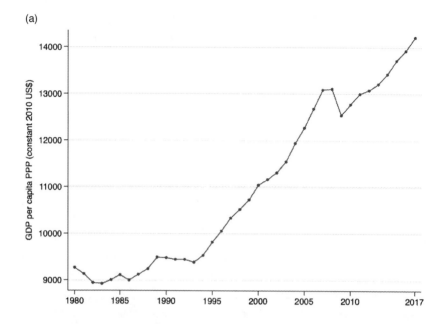

(b)

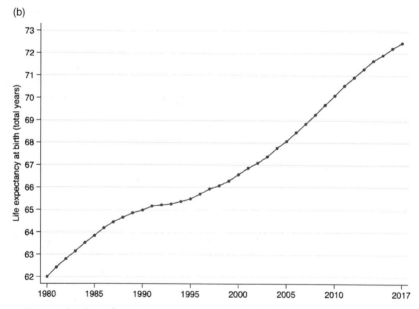

Figure 3.3 Beneficial outcomes in countries that became more capitalist

3.1.3 China's Growth Miracle

The economic history of Western European countries and other countries'
experience with socialism illustrate how economic success depends in large

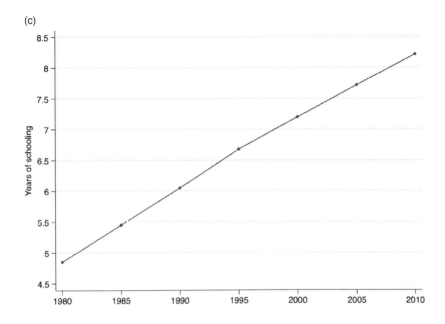

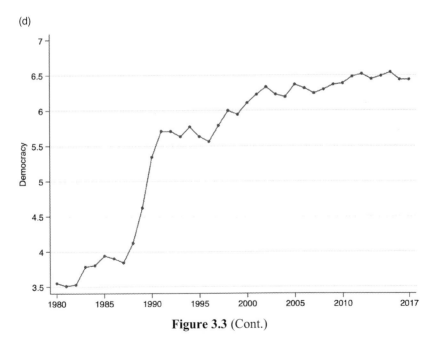

Figure 3.3 (Cont.)

measure on private property rights. China's economic reforms since 1978 have generated rapid economic growth and development, as shown in Figure 3.4. In 2010 China surpassed Japan as the world's second-largest economy.

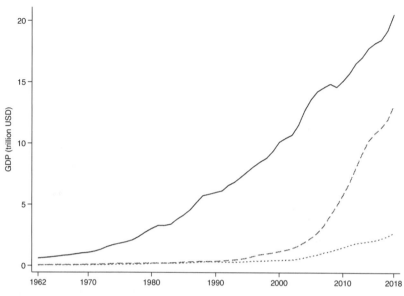

Figure 3.4 Economic growth in China

The approach to economic reforms that China has pursued is what Deng Xiaoping called "crossing the river by feeling the stones": a process that is gradual, careful, and allows trial and error. The countryside, where the reforms began, experimented with rural decollectivization, reconfiguration of land property rights, and rural industrialization, among other changes. The change from full-fledged collectivization of agricultural output to the individual-household-based farming system, now known as the Household Responsibility System (HRS), improved individual incentives and consequently contributed to a drastic growth in agricultural productivity (Lin 1992). The HRS began in 1979, at the time when only 1 percent of rural production teams adopted the HRS. The proportion increased to 98 percent by the end of 1983 and 99 percent by 1984 (ibid.). Figure 3.5 shows that the massive expansion of the HRS was associated with a rapid growth in both grain output and grain productivity.

China's economic rise also reflects increasing protection of private property. Although it took a long time, China introduced an amendment to its constitution in 2004 and passed its first Property Law in 2007, both of which formally protect private property rights. Private entrepreneurs can join the Chinese Communist Party, becoming "red capitalists" (Dickson 2003, 2008). They can protect their property rights through various political connections – for example, by becoming a local congressman (Hou 2019). In certain market areas in which laws and regulations lag behind market activities, such as e-commerce, the state allows

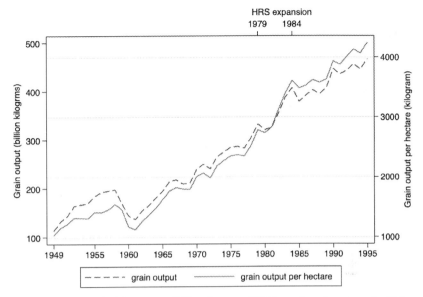

Figure 3.5 Household Responsibility System (HRS) and grain output in China

the private sector to take part in building legal infrastructure for contract enforcement, protection of property rights, and resolution of disputes. This "law, Chinese style" approach has allowed the private sector to engineer economic reforms (Liu and Weingast 2018).

One challenge in autocracies is how to tie the hands of the regime to make it credibly commit to private property rights. China has been described as a market-preserving federal system, meaning political authority is delegated to local governments to constrain predation by the central government (Montinola, Qian, and Weingast 1995, Qian and Weingast 1997). Political decentralization encourages economic competition among local governments and encourages local-government entrepreneurship (Maskin, Qian, and Xu 2000; Xu 2011). The institutionalization of the Communist Party (e.g., fixed term limits for Party and government leaders) also allows autocrats to make credible commitments to private investors (Gehlbach and Keefer 2011).

3.1.4 Property and Economic Development in Botswana and Somalia

In addition to South Korea, another country with outpaced performance compared to its neighbors is Botswana. Botswana's growth rate from 1965 to 1998 was around 7.7 percent, and in 1998, the country's per capita GDP growth rate was about ten times sub-Saharan Africa's average growth rate. This growth was surprising: When the British left, infrastructure development was limited and human-capital investment low – and the country is landlocked. Since independence, diamonds are about 40 percent of national output and though natural resources are often considered a curse, they have not been so in Botswana because property rights are secure and political decision makers face constraints (Mehlum, Moene, and Torvik 2006).

Acemoglu, Johnson, and Robinson (2003) offer an institutional explanation of Botswana's economic performance. According to them, Botswana's growth resulted from secure property rights, which in turn resulted from a combination of political and economic factors. Botswana's tribal institutions encouraged broad-based participation and constrained political leaders during the precolonial period. These institutions were only somewhat affected by British colonization because Botswana was peripheral to the empire's interests. After independence, rural chiefs and cattle owners were able to maintain political power, yet local institutions for self-governance, including the customary institution of kgotla, constrained their behavior. The result was robust private property rights for the ranching sector, enabling sustained economic growth. Table 3.1 evidences the disparities of income between sub-Saharan Africa and the rest of the world while Table 3.2 shows how well Botswana has performed compared to its neighbors.

Table 3.1 Sub-Saharan Africa in Comparative Perspective

	GDP per capita, 1998 US $	% labor force in agriculture, 1990	Life expectancy at birth, 1997
World	4,890	49	66.7
Sub-Saharan Africa	510	68	48.9

Source: Acemoglu, Johnson, and Robinson (2003)

Table 3.2 Botswana in comparative perspective

	GDP per capita, 1998 US $	% labor force in agriculture, 1990	% total pop. urban, 1970	% total pop. urban, 1998	Life expectancy at birth, 1997
Botswana	3,070	46	8	49	47
Ghana	390	59	29	37	60
Zambia	330	75	30	39	40

Source: Acemoglu, Johnson, and Robinson (2003)

The experience in Botswana can be contrasted with that in Somalia. Somalia is a predominantly nomadic and customary society. Unlike what happened in Botswana – where, Acemoglu, Johnson, and Robinson (2003) suggest, institutions encouraged cooperation between tribes – British colonial rule and Somali institutions clashed and created divisiveness, resulting in interclan competition for political control and, in turn, internecine war, government predation, and rent seeking. The result was the collapse of the Somali state in 1991.

Compared to the status quo ante, state collapse may not have been the worst thing to befall Somalia. Leeson (2007c), for example, finds that economic development actually improved after the collapse, which he primarily attributes to the removal of the predatory failed state and resurgence of clan governance. As Leeson (2007b: 690) notes, "Although a properly constrained government may be superior to statelessness, it may not be true that any government is superior to no government all."

Leeson's findings in Somalia suggest that state institutions provide a more compelling explanation for underdevelopment than the features of customary governance. And though Somalia may be better off stateless as a second-best arrangement, it is still unlikely that it will be able to realize economic growth comparable to Botswana's as Somalia remains unstable, in part because of continued foreign efforts to reinstate the state. In the meantime, customary governance provides a framework for effective governance. Table 3.3 summarizes the comparative analysis.

3.1.5 The Importance of Considering All Dimensions of Private Property Rights

The previous studies primarily focus on increases to the security of private property rights as an explanation for wealth creation. The other dimensions of a property regime – clarity of allocation, credibility of persistence, and alienability – also play an important role.

Table 3.3 Comparing Botswana and Somalia

	Botswana	**Somalia**
Economic growth	Strong	Weak
Ethnic composition	Homogeneous	Homogeneous
Political institutions	Democratic	Authoritarian
Property institutions	Private	Fragmented
Customary institutions	Strong, constrained	Strong, constrained

Source: Adapted from Acemoglu, Johnson, and Robinson (2003) and Leeson (2007c)

For example, consider Heller's (1998) exploration of the problem of the anticommons, which challenges the concept of alienability. According to Heller, the anticommons results from a multitude of rights to exclude others from the same resource; fundamentally, it is a problem of confusion about the clarity of allocation, resulting in functionally inalienable rights as no one person can make a binding decision about the use of a resource. Heller attributes the rough and often lackluster transition from socialist to market institutions to the tragedy of the anticommons. Even with the creation of private property rights, ownership was not clearly allocated.

Alienability is an important feature of a property rights regime and contributes significantly to whether the allocation of rights will be efficient. If the right to a resource is not alienable – that is, if ownership cannot be transferred to new users – then there is no possibility of exchange if another person values the right more than the current owner. If property rights are well defined, clearly allocated, and alienable, then the market will allocate property rights efficiently, provided transaction costs are not prohibitive (Coase 1960). This is the implication of the famous Coase theorem. The Coase theorem focuses attention on transaction costs (Allen 2015) – the costs of redefining and reallocating property rights (Allen 1991b). It illustrates the importance of alienability as a criterion for wealth-creating property rights: Alienable rights are necessary to achieve an efficient allocation of resources.

Another important benefit of alienability, which is a feature of an efficient allocation of rights, is that it allows for scale economies where fractionalized and inalienable holdings might not. For example, consider the importance of alienability in the nineteenth-century US context in which the BIA was tasked with allocating land to Native Americans on reservations. Allottees received only a very small fraction of land that, on its own, had little productive capacity. The BIA placed restrictions on the sale of rights to that land, resulting in low levels of production on Native American land (Leonard, Parker, and Anderson, forthcoming; McChesney 1990). Without alienable rights, those allocated land were stuck with minimally producing plots; however, if those same individuals were able to exchange their rights, the better farmers could have purchased adjacent land to their own to achieve economies of scale.

A similar explanation can be provided for why black farmers on US land were less productive than white farmers on US land or black farmers on Cherokee land. Following the Civil War, General William T. Sherman gave freed slaves in some Southern states 40 acres of land and a mule. Yet 40 acres was nowhere near enough land to compete with white farmers. If we compare black farmers' situation to the situations of white farmers, who often had at least 160 acres, or black farmers on Cherokee land, who faced no restrictions on the amount of land they could hold, it is no surprise that those with only 40 acres were far less productive (Miller 2011, forthcoming).

We have also seen in the discussion of the origins of private property rights the critical role of constraining political decision makers, which determines whether property rights are credible. When political decision makers are not constrained, the government's promise to respect property rights does not improve well-being because such a promise is not credible, and a noncredible promise is no promise at all. North and Weingast's (1989) analysis of the Glorious Revolution provides one such example. Their analysis suggests that property rights were insecure before the revolution and investment lower because of the absence of limits on the prerogative powers of the monarchy.

3.1.6 Wealth-Destroying Private Property Rights

The general trend is that the presence of secure and alienable private rights generates wealth. But this is not always the case, and establishing private rights where they do not currently exist is not a free lunch. For instance, the resources required to define and enforce an exclusive right to a resource might exceed the value of preventing the resource's overuse (Anderson and Hill 1983; Field 1989; Lueck 2002). And if private rights were extended and transaction costs were high enough to prevent a voluntary reaggregation through exchange, the social value of the private rights would be negative: They would destroy, not create, wealth.

Why would anyone engage in privatization that reduces wealth? We discuss why institutions change in Section 4, but for now, consider a theory provided by Leeson and Harris (2018b). Leeson and Harris develop what they call a "theory of wealth-destroying private rights," which recognizes the possible divergence between privatization's effect on social wealth and privatization's effect on political decision makers who decide whether to privatize a resource. As they argue, when those decision makers are residual claimants, privatization's effect on society and on the decision makers moves in the same direction. When decision makers lack claims to the residual rents of property creation, the two effects may diverge. The implication of their theory is that wealth-destroying private rights may be extended where the decision makers are able to privately benefit despite generating a negative effect for everyone else. Subsequent work of Leeson, Harris, and Myers (2020) adds to this theory by explaining how external subsidies and soft budget constraints can make decision makers non-claimants and encourage the pursuit of wealth-destroying property rights.[27]

---

[27] International aid, in such contexts where politicians are not residual claimants, is likely to increase the scope of predation by providing predatory governments with greater ability to extract property (Dutta, Leeson, and Williamson 2013; Murtazashvili and Murtazashvili 2020).

Also consider the work of Acemoglu and Johnson (2005) on the issue of granting new powers to relatively weak and predatory states to create property. Acemoglu and Johnson (2005) show that property institutions, considered as protections against state expropriation, have a first-order effect on long-run economic growth, investment, and financial development, while contracting institutions, considered as rules and regulations governing contracting between ordinary citizens, appear to only matter for financial intermediation. They posit as a possible explanation that individuals often find ways to avoid the adverse effects of weak contracting institutions but may find it more challenging to mitigate risk of expropriation by the state. Though not explicitly mentioned by the authors, one plausible implication of their finding is that when we empower states to engage in property creation to receive the benefits associated with better contracting institutions – for example, through land titling to improve credit markets or land markets – we may be opening the door for increased expropriation, which has a more direct effect on growth than weak formal contracting institutions have.

Slavery is another example of wealth-destroying private rights. The definition of slavery is private property rights over other people. And though Fogel and Engerman (1974) argue that Southern slaves encouraged production, Hummel (2013) focuses on the net losses slavery created for the Southern economy. Nunn (2008) shows that those who engaged in slavery were worse off as a result – not to mention the brutal costs to the slaves themselves.

3.1.7 Trade-Offs

Although property rights contribute to wealth creation, there may be trade-offs. Werner Troesken (2015) provides insight into some of the trade-offs for public health arising from stronger protection of property rights. Troesken's economic history of the United States recognizes that private property rights contributed to economic growth and that economic liberties can reduce the ability to provide public goods, including fighting disease. He calls this a pox of liberty. Still, as Geloso and Bologna Pavlik (forthcoming) explain using evidence from the response to the 1918 Spanish Flu pandemic, countries with greater economic freedom come out of the pandemic wealthier, which has benefits for fighting diseases that are tied to poverty.

The COVID-19 (coronavirus) pandemic further illustrates the trade-off between property protection (and economic freedom more generally) and public health. Economically free countries confront greater deaths (Geloso and Murtazashvili 2020), suggesting that some governments are simply less able to deal with pandemics because of the characteristics of their institutions.

However, in regions where property rights have been suppressed historically, especially Native American reservations, the lack of economic development arising from property insecurity contributes to less access to hospitals and many more people living in single-family homes, each exacerbating the spread of coronavirus on reservations (Crepelle and Murtazashvili 2020). Thus, it would appear that very strong or very weak property rights can contribute to worse outcomes as far as pandemics are concerned.

3.2 Property Rights and the Commons

3.2.1 The Tragedy of the Commons

The tragedy of the commons refers to the losses arising from open access to a rival resource. One reason for the tragedy is the challenge of assigning exclusive property rights, whether individual, communal, or state owned.

Many of the initial economic studies of the tragedy considered how environmental degradation relates to economic development. The theories were based on the Kuznets curve, relating economic development (measured by income or wealth) to inequality; it suggests societies start from an initial condition of inequality in agrarian and early-industrial times, which eventually declines with development before increasing again (Kuznets 1955). Subsequent studies applied the same logic to the environment and suggested that pollution and overuse of the commons, such as forests, increase with industrialization and then declines at higher levels of economic development once society is wealthy enough to bear the cost of property creation and more restrictive use of these resources (Stern 2004).

Unfortunately, there is not much empirical support for the environmental Kuznets curve – both because wealthy countries do not always reduce pollution as expected and because lower-income countries can adopt strategies and technologies to abate pollution to a greater extent than the theory predicts (Choumert, Motel, and Dakpo 2013). This is not wholly surprising because the theory leaves out institutions.[28] Instead, if we wish to understand governance of the commons and the prevention of the tragedy of the commons, a better starting point is Elinor Ostrom (1990) and her exploration of property rights institutions.

3.2.2 Governance of the Commons

Ostrom (1990) begins her work by examining the game-theoretic logic behind the tragedy of the commons. "What makes these models so dangerous," she

---

[28] So too does the standard Kuznets curve. As Acemoglu and Robinson (2002) point out, political institutions ultimately determine how economic growth influences inequality.

argues, "is that the constraints that are assumed to be fixed for the purpose of analysis are taken on faith as being fixed in empirical settings" (Ostrom 1990: 6). What she sets out to do instead is "address the question of how to enhance the capabilities of those involved to change the constraining rules of the game to lead to outcomes other than remorseless tragedies" (Ostrom 1990: 7). This pursuit culminates in her eight design principles for effective governance, which are listed in Figure 3.6.

The first of these design principles acknowledges the importance of boundaries to internalize the externalities associated with an unregulated commons: The resource needs to be made exclusive. Cheung (1970), for example, showed that clarifying boundaries can align private and social costs of extraction. Yet clarifying boundaries does not automatically result in social harmony. In fact, the opposite may be the case, as establishing boundaries often results in conflict (see Section 4.3 for an extended discussion) over how boundaries assign rights over future value streams (Libecap 1989b). Boundary clarification may also contribute to vulnerability. For example, nomadic pastoral communities may depend on fluid property rights, and clarification efforts may reduce their access to pasture (Lesorogol 2005; see also Leeson and Harris 2018b). Nevertheless, for effective governance of the commons, establishing exclusive boundaries is essential and the first step toward avoiding tragedy.

The second design principle states that there should be both congruence between costs incurred and benefits received and flexibility based on changes in conditions. For example, it may make sense to allow communities to reallocate property rights in response to community-wide crises, such as a drought or a flood. Such flexibility reduces security of individual property rights, but such

Figure 3.6 Design principles for effective self-governing property regimes

P1: Well-defined boundaries around a community of users and the resources
P2: Congruence between appropriation and provision rules and local conditions
P3: Participatory collective-choice arrangements
P4: Presence of monitors who are members of and accountable to the community
P5: Graduated sanctions for violations of community norms
P6: Low-cost and accessible conflict-resolution mechanisms
P7: Minimum recognition of community rights to organize by external government bodies
P8: Governance activities nested in multiple, nested enterprises

Source: Adapted from Ostrom (1990)

reallocation may be a useful form of social insurance that improves community well-being.

According to the third design principle, inclusive collective-choice arrangements can provide knowledge of local conditions at low cost but can also be co-opted or dominated by powerful individuals. Thus, it is necessary to consider the diversity of collective decision-making arrangements at the local level, with special attention to the fact that even local governments are subject to political-market failures (Acemoglu, Reed, and Robinson 2014; Agrawal and Gibson 1999; Boettke, Coyne, and Leeson 2011).

The fourth design principle recognizes the importance of monitoring members' use and of monitors being members of the community or directly accountable to members of the community. Beyond Ostrom's case studies, other empirical examples illustrate the importance of monitors' accountability. For instance, when guards are hired locally, they are more accountable and resource governance improves (Chhatre and Agrawal 2008). According to the fifth principle, proportionality in sanctions (the idea that the punishment fits the crime) can improve the legitimacy and hence effectiveness of the communal property arrangements. The sixth principle recognizes that local conflict-resolution mechanisms are more likely to succeed in addressing disputes over resource use than centralized ones, especially in contexts in which formal legal institutions are costly to use or corrupt.

Ostrom (1990: 14–15) is explicit in her rejection of the "sterile dichotomy" between the market and the state as the only solution to tragedy. Her design principles for enduring self-governance leave an explicit role for the state, even if that role is largely to back off. The seventh design principle clarifies the importance of polycentricity for successful self-governance, the defining feature of which is local autonomy and rights to organize. The importance of polycentric governance and autonomy was also solidified empirically. Every community that Ostrom (1990: 180) studied in which the right to self-govern was challenged by external authority resulted in weak or failed institutional performance. Principle seven acknowledges that the state's efforts to impose rules on communities can set the society back. Subsequent work on criminal or otherwise-illegal communities (Harris 2018; Leeson 2008; Skarbek 2016) tries to test the robustness of the design principles by analyzing situations in which illegality prevents the recognized right to govern from being secured.

The final design principle emphasizes the importance of horizontal linkages (with other informal and self-governing organizations) and the relationships between self-governing communities and different levels of government. When government often fails to respect rights, communities may choose anarchy as an escape from the predatory state (Scott 1999, 2009). Vertical linkages can improve the state's commitment to recognizing common property.

Ostrom's subsequent work developed a more complex framework to analyze how the social and biophysical systems interact to explain governance of the commons (E. Ostrom 2009; E. Ostrom, Janssen, and Anderies 2007). These perspectives also include the ways in which social capital, including trust and social networks, influence collective action (E. Ostrom and Ahn 2009). McGinnis (2011) summarizes the institutional analysis and development (IAD) framework, and Cole, Epstein, and McGinnis (2019) explain how the IAD and social-ecological systems (SES) frameworks can be combined. In reviewing the empirical work and case studies that stemmed from Ostrom's research, Cox, Arnold, and Tomás (2010) find that the design principles have much support.

A related literature comes from the contracting approach to governance of the commons. For example, consider Gary Libecap, James Smith, and Steve Wiggins's work on property rights to oil and gas reservoirs.[29] Their research focuses on unitization: an agreement by well operators to share in the collective fruits of what the reservoir produces. Unitization is a contractual arrangement that reduces losses associated with common pool extraction, although implementing it has not always been smooth. Many parties resist unitizing reservoirs and thereby assigning field operations to a single firm with all others holding shares in the net revenues of production, and negotiation can take years. To facilitate agreement, unitization contracts often distinguish between multiple participating areas or time phases of production in assigning property rights. In the face of contracting problems, state governments have adopted legislation to force unitization via majority rules.

The effective governance of the commons can also depend on the presence of well-functioning markets. Cowen and Delmotte (2021) consider a meta-governance problem: What governance process should decide the size and scope of institutions to govern the commons? They explain why a bottom-up response to problems of mismatched property rights is facilitated in societies characterized by market processes. Market processes are important to deliver price signals to local communities, including essential knowledge about the cost of maintaining private property rights and the relative scarcity of communal goods. A related approach is offered by Hill (2014), who argues that bison on the US frontier were brought nearly to extinction not because of incomplete property rights but because the land buffalo roamed was more valuable for settlement and railroads. He argues that when the value of buffalo increased

---

[29] See Libecap and Wiggins (1985), Wiggins and Libecap (1985), and Libecap and Smith (1999, 2002).

because of scarcity, individuals invested resources to conserve them. Another meta-approach, robust political economy (Pennington 2013), combines the best of Austrian and public choice insights to emphasize both the information and incentive problems involved in common pool resource governance.

3.2.3 The Radio Spectrum

One famous example of a commons problem solved through a combination of property rights and government action is the radio spectrum in the United States. According to Hazlett (2017), the popular perception is that before the Federal Communications Commission (FCC) in 1927, the radio spectrum was open access, with significant conflicts over who had use rights to the valuable parts of the spectrum. Through the FCC, the regulatory system assigned and allocated property rights, but it did so through a bureaucratic system that required the government to determine the prices of property rights to the spectrum. Such a system may have been more effective than open access, but perhaps there was an even better method of allocation.

Enter Ronald Coase, who explained that bureaucratic allocation undermined the efficiency of the spectrum and offered the solution of auctioning off the spectrum rights. The government took Coase's advice. The creation of a market to rights to the spectrum increased government revenue and enhanced the efficiency of the allocation of property rights (Coase 2013).

Not everyone accepts that the influence of Coase on the FCC led to a happy conclusion. Hazlett (2017), for example, considers the resulting property rights regime to be more reflective of powerful group interests than private, competitive markets. Hazlett sees it as a story of regulatory capture in which lobbying presented challenges and resulted in inefficiency, even if credit for reform rightfully goes to Coase.

Beyond these considerations, an emerging literature considers how technology creates the possibility of fully decentralized spectrum governance. Bustamante et al. (2020), combining insights from Leeson's (2014a) analysis of anarchy; Boettke, Coyne, and Leeson's (2011) theory of quasi-market failure; research on the innovation commons (Potts 2019); and Elinor Ostrom's (1990) research on commons governance, refer to the emergent approach as spectrum anarchy. This approach focuses on how artificial intelligence can allow fully decentralized governance of spectrum to enable more rapid adaptation to changes in conditions. It thus offers an example of Posner and Weyl's (2017, 2018) notion of radical markets, in which any property rights arrangement creates monopoly rights that may undermine welfare-improving opportunities for reallocating rights. In the case of spectrum governance, technology promises even more rapid adaptation to changes in local conditions than Coasean markets for spectrum rights.

3.2.4 Commons at Scale

The standard solution to the tragedy of the commons is to establish private property rights over the resource. However, as Hardin (1968: 1245) suggests, not every resource can "readily be fenced." Oceans and space are important examples of commons that illustrate that privatization does not always make economic sense – at least not with the given technology.

One possible way to govern the oceans is privatization (for example, Block and Nelson 2015). To prevent the erosion of the Great Barrier Reef and the possible extinction of a tremendous number of species, we could establish private rights to portions of the reef such that the various owners would have an economic incentive to maintain their value. But such a solution largely depends on the costs of excluding nonauthorized users. Because the barrier reef is tremendously expansive – not to mention being in the ocean - exclusion would be costly. Would the cost of depleting the reef exceed the technical costs required to establish and enforce individual ownership claims to it? Perhaps, but it would likely require a third party to overcome the negotiating costs required to establish property rights in such a situation. Further, it is likely that because of the scale, it would be even lower cost for the third party, the government, to establish state ownership and regulate public use (even with the inability to rationally calculate and even with the potential for selective enforcement and predation).

Once a third party is required to enforce rights at scale, the question becomes whether private property rights or regulated state ownership would be more appropriate. Bromley (2008, 2009a), for example, questions the logic of privatization, in part because regulated state ownership of such resources has been shown to work effectively at scale. Despite these considerations, where exclusion is possible, such as with fisheries closer to the shore – and hence less costly to privatize – private property rights are associated with tremendous reductions in depletion of the world's ocean fisheries (Costello, Gaines, and Lynham 2008; Worm et al. 2009).

Space is another commons at a massive scale. One possibility is allocating private property rights in space through first possession, which could encourage exploration. However, there may be substantial costs of enforcing these rights, and, as with the ocean, the extent to which the evolution of spontaneous economic rights makes sense depends on the benefits and costs of enforcement (Salter and Leeson 2014). An alternative method is to establish space as a common heritage of humankind, which is a collective property right

(Buxton 2004). The question, however, is whether such a system would lead to de facto open access and eventual tragedy.

Anderson and Hill's (2001) work on technology and property suggests that in both situations, the best we can hope for is some change in the technology of enforcement that allows for a low-cost way to align incentives and internalize the externalities. Encouraging such a development might first require the promise of return, perhaps through committing to allow the inventors to claim the resource through first possession.

3.2.5 Pollution, Climate Change, and the Global Commons

An issue related to governance of the ocean or space is governance of the climate and planet more generally. As Stavins (2011) suggests, the carrying capacity of the planet is more of a problem for open-access resources for which there is no clear property right, the planet as a whole included. As with any open-access common pool resource – only now on a planetary scale – individuals, communities, and nations have incentives to free ride on the contribution of others to such goods as abatement of pollution and abatement of overfishing the oceans (Barrett 2010; E. Ostrom al. 1999). Whereas the standard solutions of the market (private property rights), the state (state ownership and public regulation), or even Ostrom-style self-governance may work well at a scale at which monitoring and enforcing behavior are feasible, the challenge of global collective-action problems such as climate change is that a solution necessarily involves multiple parties, policies, and scales of governance (Aldy, Barrett, and Stavins 2003; E. Ostrom 2010b).

That does not mean that property rights do not have a role to play in such global tragedies. Economists and policy makers increasingly agree that one part of the solution to pollution involves some version of a cap-and-trade policy, with international coordination to address the challenge of pollution havens (Barrett and Stavins 2003). Such a policy can help internalize at least some of the externalities associated with pollution as it creates tradable markets in property rights and forces people to bear part of the social costs of their actions.[30] In addition, reforestation, which depends squarely on establishing excludable property rights, reduces pressure on the Earth's atmosphere.

3.3 Knowledge Commons

The knowledge-commons framework extends the idea of the resource commons to new commons, including knowledge-related domains such as

---

[30] Anderson and Libecap (2014) provide an overview of the case for markets.

innovation (Allen and Potts 2016; Potts 2018, 2019). Knowledge commons such as Wikipedia have profound effects, including the shaping of science (see Thompson and Hanley 2018). Yet, as Hess and Ostrom (2007) explain, knowledge, like any commons, is associated with social dilemmas such as underproduction, free riding, overconsumption and withdrawal of information, enclosure, inequitable access, and congestion. According to Frischmann, Madison, and Strandburg (2014), the knowledge-commons framework is a method for researching "constructed cultural commons," which is shorthand for shared resources that are products of the human mind. Knowledge refers to intellectual, informational, scientific, technical, and cultural resources. A commons is an institutional arrangement for governing shared resources used by a community of people. Community self-governance, which is often linked to other formal and informal governance mechanisms, is a key feature of the knowledge commons. The knowledge commons is thus institutionalized community governance of shared intellectual and cultural resources.

The standard economic view is that without property rights, people might not generate knowledge. The public choice and institutional economics literatures, especially that coming out of the Bloomington School, suggest otherwise (Dourado and Tabarrok 2015; Safner 2016). Madison, Frischmann, and Strandburg (2009) explain the sustainability of "commons-based peer production" in open-source software production and Wikipedia – contexts of community self-governance in which establishing property rights is challenging. In the property rights approach, intellectual property (IP) objects such as patented inventions and copyrighted works are modeled as public goods, with the standard prescription that creating marketable property rights for individuals will encourage improvements in the governance of the commons. Yet, as Madison, Frischmann, and Strandburg (2009) explain, institutions such as universities have existed for centuries based on the foundation of knowledge sharing, which suggests that openly accessible knowledge commons do not necessarily result in tragic outcomes.

Analysis of a knowledge commons begins with a description of the social dilemma(s) posed by the knowledge or information resources, including their governance – both internal governance (as exemplified by stories told by members in the community) and external governance, such as commons' relationship to IP law. It then asks whether the resource is protected either by a patent or other property right or by a legal regime of formal or informal openness (for example, in the case of public-domain information). Sometimes property rights can exacerbate commons problems, such as when a programmer secures a property right automatically by making an original contribution. Governance regimes may also entail sharing of information. Additional questions include what resources are required to produce knowledge, including the distribution of those resources; what the objectives of knowledge-commons governance are; and the extent to which openness is desired in the governance of knowledge.

Harris (2018) provides further insight into the governance of the knowledge commons by analyzing online piracy communities. Piracy is a property rights issue. Rather than simply weakening property rights, these communities govern the knowledge commons.

3.4 Property Rights and Political Order

The structure of property rights has long been associated with the political order, with causal claims made in both directions. Section 2 primarily dealt with the way the political order influences the structure of property. Here we consider how the property rights structure can alter politics. The most obvious example of how the property rights structure might affect politics comes from Karl Marx and his belief that private property rights over the means of production result in exploitation and ultimately to revolutionary pressure. Another example comes from Barrington Moore (1966), who believed that inequality in ownership is a primary source of political conflict. This theme is extended in Samuel Huntington's *Political Order in Changing Societies* (1968), in which he hypothesized that revolution is likely if not inevitable when the conditions confronting peasants are inequitable.

One resource of major political importance is land. A system with inequitable landholdings has several significant political consequences. The primary direct effect of the inequality is land grievances – claims of injustice relating to one's property – which Klaus and Mitchell (2015) show are related to electoral violence: Elections are more likely to trigger violence when they are held in a context in which large numbers of people have land grievances. Another result is a growing sense of state illegitimacy. The person who the state says owns the land and who the state is willing to back in a conflict often has the economic property right as well. Inequality in landholdings is thus often a result of state action and in some cases is created intentionally as a direct instrument of control (Anderson 1974; Tilly 1990; Wittfogel 1957). A state that sanctions and enforces a deliberate policy of inequitable distribution will often become an illegitimate one when grievances increase. Grievance-based protests and perceived state illegitimacy can result in decreased productivity, which can further undermine the state: Less productivity often means less tax revenue and thus fewer public goods – goods that can promote improvements to the political order. The result of severe inequality in landholdings is often, as Moore (1966) and Huntington (1968) suggest, political conflict and a weak or failed state.

Another mechanism through which property rights, or the lack thereof, can influence the political sphere is property insecurity's effect on political violence, terrorism, and insurgency. Rules that encourage people to beat their swords into plowshares do so by increasing the opportunity cost of participating in unproductive, violent activities (Grossman and Kim 1995). In contrast, as we have discussed, insecure property rights reduce productivity, as the owners' uncertainty over whether they will retain their use rights incentivizes them to use the resources immediately and discourages long-term investment and conservation. As a result of being unproductive, insecure rights lower the opportunity cost of engaging in violence and terrorism, as a person has less to lose and more to be angry about. Hernando de Soto (2002: xiii), for example, argues that one of the main reasons for the Maoist insurgency in Peru is that the government did not recognize the property rights of the poor. According to de Soto, "If governments do not take [the poor] seriously as economic agents, if governments see them only as a nuisance or passive recipients of charity, the resentment among the poor against the status quo will only increase. Enter the terrorists, eager to exploit the hostility against the state, encouraging the poor to focus on their exclusion rather than on their aspirations to resemble the affluent citizens of the market democracies of the West."

Empirical evidence supports this theoretical link between land governance and violence. This includes studies of the link between violence in Colombia and the inequity of land distribution (Albertus and Kaplan 2013; Steele 2011), studies about how contentious land issues induce electoral violence in sub-Saharan Africa (Benjaminsen et al. 2009; Boone 2013; Horowitz and Klaus 2018; Klaus 2020), and many others. One implication is that providing a more equitable distribution of ownership opportunities could result in quiescence. It could also result in a more stable and legitimate political order. Land grievances and political conflict are often intimately related, with land conflicts often resulting in electoral violence (Boone 2009, 2013). Using a wealth of evidence from Kenya, Klaus (2020) shows that violence is coproduced by elites and society as inequality forms the basis of contentious narratives, which are then used by elites to mobilize groups with grievances and stoke conflict.

Related to Section 3.2, this perspective provides another possible benefit of communal landholding relative to individual landholding. According to Guardado (2018), the size of ownership claims is important. An arrangement with small, individual holdings relative to one with large, communal holdings limits landholders' ability to spread risk (McCloskey 1991; Nugent and Sanchez 1993). Accordingly, small landowners are often more exposed to price volatility than people participating in communal or sharecropping arrangements. Elinor Ostrom's work anticipates such findings, as it recognizes that when property rights can adjust in response to shocks, they are better able to provide institutional solutions to vulnerability. De Soto's (2000) work, which suggests a single solution – legal recognition – does not.

4. Change in Property Rights

4.1 The Debate over Institutional Change

Scholars agree far less on the process of changing property rights institutions than on the origins or consequences of these institutions. Once we identify which property institutions are associated with wealth creation, a natural question is why everyone had not adopted the wealth-enhancing change (Weimer 1997). Considering much of the literature presented in Section 3, why doesn't every country adopt secure private property rights and a constrained, neutral third-party state? Two perspectives on institutional change offer two plausible answers: (1) The change would not actually be wealth enhancing, and, until the initial conditions and constraints change, it is efficient to not adopt the new property institution; (2) institutions do not always change in the direction of wealth maximization.

Theories of institutional change can be divided into efficiency and predatory perspectives.[31] The central idea of efficiency perspectives is that individuals and groups choose institutions that enable them to increase net social benefits. Predatory perspectives see institutional change as a process in which individuals and groups invest resources to reallocate existing benefits and to capture benefits for themselves. According to the predatory view, much institutional change involves destruction of wealth (Vahabi 2020). Whereas voluntary exchange is a common feature of the efficiency perspective, coercion figures more prominently in the predatory theory (Vahabi 2015).

4.2 Efficiency Perspectives

Efficiency as a mechanism of institutional change is most commonly associated with Coase (1960) and Demsetz (1967). Coase argues that individuals bargain over property rights in ways that are efficient provided property rights are clearly delineated and transaction costs are reasonably low. This idea was initially formalized by George Stigler as the Coase theorem, which Allen (2015: 379) restates as follows: "If transaction costs are zero, then the allocation

---

[31] Both perspectives go by many names. See Leeson and Harris (2018a) for just some of the terms used to refer to these two perspectives.

of resources is independent of the distribution of property rights." With Coasean bargaining, the allocation and structure of property rights changes to reflect who values them the most, resulting in an efficient allocation of resources. Similarly, in Demsetz's (1967: 350) theory of property rights, "the emergence of new property rights takes place in response to the desires of the interacting persons for adjustment to new benefit-cost possibilities ... [from] changes in technology and relative prices." The central prediction of Coase's and Demsetz's positions is that a change in institutions will result in an increase in social wealth; otherwise, such a change will not occur.

Similar treatments of institutional change can be found in many seminal works on property rights. For instance, consider North and Thomas's (1973) treatment of the motivation for institutional change:

> The economic logic of institutional change can be stated as follows: institutional arrangements which increase efficiency will not be set up unless the private benefits of their creation exceed the costs.

Or Barzel's (2002: 4–5):

> Individuals will always choose institutions to maximize wealth, subject to the costs of transacting.

Leeson (2020; italics in original) puts it this way:

> Maximization implies efficiency, *always and everywhere*, because maximizers maximize, *always and everywhere*.

In other words, we should not call observed institutions inefficient, for until the real costs of changing institutions change, all existing institutions are efficient.

The efficiency perspective suggests that the property regime is chosen optimally in response to transaction costs, which implies that supposedly wealth-maximizing property rights do not emerge because they are not wealth-enhancing when we consider the costs of establishing them. Alternatively, a property regime emerges or changes if the emergence or change is on net beneficial.

4.3 Predatory Perspectives

Predatory perspectives place conflict at the center of institutional change. Vahabi (2015), for example, views the process of institutional change as a struggle between predators with power and their potential prey. Accordingly, institutional change is governed by efforts of groups to dominate one another, and, as a result, the creation and allocation of property rights may reflect differentials in power dynamics rather than wealth-enhancing exchanges and efficiency (Vahabi 2004, 2016). The general prediction of a predatory theory of institutional change is that such change disproportionately benefits those with more power, often at the expense of those with less.

Several specific mechanisms contribute to or constitute predation:

- Differential bargaining power between groups (Knight 1992)
- Rent seeking: the investment of scarce resources to secure benefits from government (Krueger 1974; Tullock 1967)
- Political and bureaucratic interests in the absence of political constraints (Boettke and Candela 2020)

Whereas the efficiency perspective, likely because of its association with Demsetz (1967), is commonly associated with economic property rights, the mechanisms of predatory change are often associated with legal property rights. Because legal property rights depend on the scope of the state, more powerful groups and those better able to seek rents are typically able to influence the process of change in legal property rights, which then can result in changes to the economic rights. Consider land formalization in Colombia. A large portion of the land in Colombia is held informally. Yet those whose claims are legally recognized oppose further extension of formal rights to those who currently lack them because the extension would devalue their own property (Ferrell 2019).

In many instances, it is those within the government who have the greatest ability to engage in predation, and it is not uncommon for the government to invest significant resources to capture land and revenue. Accordingly, Vahabi (2011, 2016) suggests that resources that are easy to expropriate are protected by relatively insecure property rights whereas secure property rights are more likely to emerge for resources that are difficult for the government to expropriate. Human capital, for example, is a resource that is very difficult for governments to control because the prey (humans) are often able to avoid capture. The state is thus more likely to assert ownership over capturable assets. This claim is also illustrated by the work of Scott (2009), who documents how the ability of people to hide their assets shapes how well they are able to evade state predation.

The predatory perspective suggests that property rights institutions reflect the interests of powerful groups in society. In this regard, the perspective underlies the theories of selective enforcement discussed in Section 2.3. A selective-enforcement regime is simply the outcome of the conflict over property and rents, with the more powerful victors gaining or maintaining control over resources (often) at the expense of others. What causes an institutional change from this perspective is not a change in enforcement technologies, relative prices, or even the available rent to be distributed; instead, institutions change when people fight over those rents. So property rights may change in a direction that is wealth destroying rather than wealth enhancing, as those with power capture gains for themselves while imposing costs on others. Rather than sharing in rent creation, people fight and seek rents, increasing their private returns but reducing the total level of wealth in society.

The problem the predatory perspective identifies is that once power enters the scene, the Coase theorem – a mechanism by which wealth-enhancing exchanges occur and property rights get allocated efficiently to those with the highest-valued use – cannot function as well. The seeming lack of a political Coase theorem allows an inefficient, wealth-destroying property regime to emerge and be maintained. And, unless the polity can solve the commitment problem identified in Section 2.2, property may go to the predator.

4.4 Reconciling the Debate

The two perspectives are often treated as being at odds with one another (see Heritier 2007; Tang 2011) as each generates a different set of primary predictions: If an institutional change does not disproportionately benefit those with power, the predatory perspective seems an unlikely candidate to be able to explain the change; if an institutional change results in a net loss and reduces overall social wealth, then the efficiency perspective seems inapplicable. Yet the two are perhaps more related than one might think, and it is not difficult to reconcile the two theories. Even early proponents of the predatory perspective, such as Knight (1992), Knight and Sened (1995), and Knight and North (1997), are careful to suggest that the two are not mutually exclusive. An efficient institutional change that increases social wealth may disproportionately benefit those with power. Provided the gains exceed the losses, it is an efficient change and a Pareto improvement.

For an example, consider the Olsonian theory of the state and property rights, discussed in Section 2 (see McGuire and Olson 1996; Olson 1993). The more powerful roving bandits become stationary to maximize their plunder; they use their strength and power to change the institutional structure in a way that allows them to capture wealth. Once stationary, the bandits are incentivized to protect their producers from plunder by other bandits and to provide public goods, such as property protection. Other, less powerful bandits lose in this situation, as might producers whose rights were initially protected because political decision makers may subsequently perceive they can gain from plundering them. Some producers may even be made worse off by the choice of the bandits to become stationary, yet still the institutional change increases social wealth on net; it is an efficient institutional change instigated by predatory methods.

Leeson and Harris (2018a), who argue that the two perspectives are complementary, suggest that even if one wants to consider the perspectives as separate, competing explanations, empirically adjudicating between them to explain an institutional change is not as simple as it seems: Finding evidence for one perspective does not speak to the salience of the other. Evidencing the benefits to those with power says nothing about the net effects of the resulting change; similarly, identifying losses does not provide evidence of lack of gains elsewhere.

4.5 Evolutionary Perspectives, or Why Property Is "Always Becoming"

A more meta approach to institutional change can be found in evolutionary economics, which is its own subfield within the field of institutional economics.[32] Whether the impetus for institutional change is conflict or reward does not matter; what matters is that things change and respond to change in an evolutionary fashion. Much of modern evolutionary economics builds on work from Hayek's *The Fatal Conceit.* In it, Hayek (1988) explains how the rules we live by were never designed, nor do we fully understand their function. The spontaneously emergent institutional structure allows us to use dispersed and tacit knowledge, yet the transmission mechanism cannot necessarily be known or articulated: "Such new rules would spread not because men understood that they were more effective, or could calculate that they would lead to expansion, but simply because they enabled those groups practicing them to procreate more successfully and to include outsiders." Hayek does not claim to understand when cultural evolution began, but somehow over time, orderly cooperation was extended and "common concrete ends were replaced by general, end-independent abstract rules of conduct."[33] These rules were the foundation of the Great Society.

Much of Hayek's institutional and evolutionary work speaks to the emergence and change of institutions broadly, but Hayek (1988: 34–38) discusses the nature of property specifically. In *The Fatal Conceit*, he recounts classical liberal perspectives on private property rights, such as those of Adam Smith, who believed private property rights are what separate man from beast; Locke, who thought that there can be no justice without recognition of private property rights; and Montesquieu, who believed that commerce and property are what spread civilization and sweet manners to the barbarians of Northern Europe.

---

[32] See especially Hodgson (1996, 2007) on the economics of evolution.
[33] See also Belloc and Bowles (2013, 2017) on the persistence of wealth-destroying cultures.

Although Hayek (1988: 36) undoubtedly expresses similar sentiments, he also recognizes the limits of our ability to design property: "While property is initially a product of custom, and jurisdiction and legislation have merely developed it in the course of millennia, there is then no reason to suppose that the particular forms it has assumed in the contemporary world are final. Traditional concepts of property rights have in recent times been recognized as a modifiable and very complex bundle whose most effective combinations have not yet been discovered in all areas." It is this view that differentiates Hayek's theories of property from the earlier theories. Classical liberals tended to view property in a fixed form, while Hayek recognized that property is continually evolving; it is, to use a phrase that institutionalists have used to describe the economy, always becoming.

4.6 Polycentricism, Efficient Redaction, and Experimentation in Property Rights

Even if property institutions emerge spontaneously, political (or designed) order still plays a role. Accordingly, it is necessary to articulate a political theory to understand how governance institutions contribute to the evolution of property rights institutions. Polycentrism provides a possibly useful link between the theory of spontaneous order in markets and the evolution of legal rules. Polycentrism – which refers to power sharing, and not simply decentralization of decision making – provides a foundation for the experimentation that Hayek understood to be important to the evolution of property rights.

Polycentrism allows for – one might even say requires – experimentation. Accordingly, it can provide a framework for more efficient redaction – the process of assembling different spontaneous property institutions into one coherent legal framework. Because formalization of property rights may fail to maximize wealth, what is needed is a political process by which the legal recognition of informal rights can occur at multiple, overlapping, and even redundant levels. Experimenting before imposing a legal framework at scale allows us to learn the best way to recognize and coalesce divergent spontaneous property institutions.

Part of the credit for China's successful economic reform should be given to policy experimentation at the local level. The HRS, the Chinese system that permits family farming to replace collective farming, began in Anhui Province. The HRS reform is but one example of local policy experimentation at the local level. Special economic zones introduced a new set of rules (for example, secure property rights, preferential policies, streamlined administrative procedures) first in four cities in Guangdong and Fujian Provinces – two provinces close to Hong Kong and Taiwan, respectively – to attract foreign investment. Township village enterprises (TVEs) – enterprises owned by townships or village collectives – prospered in southern Jiangsu Province and led rural industrialization in China (Oi 1999). Wenzhou, a city in Zhejiang province, known as "the bastion of Chinese capitalism" (Huang 2008, 58), witnessed vibrant development of the private sector (when the predominant economic form was public elsewhere in China) despite formal constraints on capitalism. The private sector gradually developed by relying on informal finance and disguising its private ownership by registering enterprises as TVEs, a strategy called "wearing a red hat." These informal coping strategies, or adaptive informal institutions (Tsai 2007), constitute experimentation under hierarchy in China (Heilmann 2008). The resulting formalizations constituted arguably efficiency-enhancing redactions.

The economic history of mining in the United States also provides an example of this type of process. Miners occupied land from 1848 to 1849. By 1866, Congress responded with a general Mining Act that redacted the informal rules. The congressional response recognized that the formal rules Congress had created for allocation of land in the American West were not suited for the miners' needs and that policy makers in Washington, DC, thousands of miles from the frontier and often with no experience in the West, could do no better than what the miners had learned to do. The legal regime of 1866 provided the basis for mining regulation for the next century and beyond (Murtazashvili 2017). It would not have done so if it had not been based on local experience.

5. Property Rights and Development Policy

5.1 Land Redistribution

One of the conclusions of the analysis so far is that private property rights and limited government are associated with economic growth and development. Yet, as we discussed with wealth-destroying private rights and predatory theories of institutional change, this is not always the case. Perhaps, then, other presumptions about the efficiency of specific institutional arrangements also need to be reconsidered. Consider the general idea of market distribution and allocation. Markets tend to allocate resources to their highest-valued use, an outcome implied by both the Coase theorem and standard competition theory. Does it ever make sense to counter the market distribution by forcibly redistributing the rights to a resource? Given that forced redistribution requires state coercion to expropriate a resource from one party to transfer it to another, it might seem obvious that, by introducing uncertainty into ownership, it would always be a bad idea.

The economic answer, as always, is that it depends.[34] On what? Like all claimed inefficiencies or problems, it depends on the costs that make it difficult for Coasean bargains to occur: transaction costs. Forced redistribution undoubtedly comes with a cost, but the relevant question is when the accompanying benefit outweighs it. The most powerful economic justification for land redistribution is severe landholding inequality, namely land oligopolies, with high transaction costs preventing sales. Land oligopolies are generally associated with lower levels of productivity (Bardhan 1973), primarily because of the costs of monitoring agents. A land oligopoly generally involves a few principals with a lot of agents who work the land. The more agents employed on the land and the fewer the principals, the costlier it becomes to monitor agents' behavior to prevent shirking. Where high transaction costs prevent the voluntary breakup and sale of the land to more owners, forcibly breaking up a land oligopoly and redistributing it for private use can push everyone out of a suboptimal equilibrium and improve incentives for productive land use. In the ideal case, the initial breakup of large landholdings would be accompanied by the free exchange of land rights and allow for productive operations at scale. Absent such free exchange, the pendulum can swing too far, as the large literature on the economic costs of fractionalized private property rights shows (Dippel and Frye 2019; Frye 2016; Miller, forthcoming). Also consider that the US federal government reallocated land from Native Americans in response to demand for white settlement. This suggests a more fundamental problem with land redistribution: It is often motivated by ideology or rent seeking.

For two reasons, real cases may come up short of this ideal. One is the Austrian emphasis on knowledge and information. The other is the public choice emphasis on incentives. In other words, even if the situation could be improved through forced redistribution, should we expect the actually existing government to both know the proper distribution and have the incentive to act to realize that distribution? It seems doubtful, particularly in a country with severe inequalities of landownership. The case for forced redistribution also ignores the alternative ways to push people out of equilibrium in the presence of high transaction costs, including reducing transaction costs through providing a stable and secure legal regime.

In some contexts, the market solves the problem of land oligopolies. In the United States during the nineteenth century, speculators often purchased large

---

[34] Harry Truman once quipped, "Give me a one-handed economist! All my economists say, 'on one hand . . . on the other.'" Although admittedly this can be frustrating, especially for those primarily interested in economics for policy conclusions, it nonetheless is the result of an important economic insight that cannot be dispensed of: "There are no solutions. There are only trade-offs."

amounts of land. But squatters occupied land in large numbers, and Congress eventually capitulated to the squatters' demands. This eliminated the chance that land oligopolies would be established outside of plantations in the South.

China's rapid urbanization can be understood as a process of land redistribution in which land has been transferred from rural households to urban land users. The distorted land markets create strong incentives for local governments to expropriate rural land, even though doing so has intensified the tension between local governments and rural households. Land-dispossessed rural households use a variety of means (for example, petition, protests, violence) to lodge their grievances about land expropriation (Sargeson 2012, 2013). Their action, individually or collectively, sometimes brings concessions from the state but does not lead to the creation of legal rights (Heurlin 2016). China currently still lacks rule of law in the Hayekian sense of clear rules enforced by the government. Rather, rules are designed in a way that gives the state the authority to legally discriminate against rural land users. To ease the tension arising from land expropriation, local governments exercise their ability to provide land-dispossessed rural households with additional compensation (Cai, Liu, and Wang 2020). They can also sugarcoat the bitter pill of land expropriation by reducing the price gap between compensation and the land's market value and by improving land governance (Cai et al. 2020).

5.2 Land Titling

A much less controversial policy to encourage development is formalizing informal property rights through legal titling. Legal titling refers to the creation of legal property rights through a formal, judicial process. The hope is that by getting registered, informal land holdings can obtain the security that a legal property regime enforces at scale. Formally identifying traditional and customary property claims and registering them within a single repository serve the dual purpose of providing a mechanism for collateralizing resources to encourage investment and providing a tax registry, the latter of which is considered necessary for the state to provide infrastructure and other public goods.

Probably the most famous proponent of legal titling is Hernando de Soto. According to de Soto (2000), underdevelopment cannot be caused by cultural differences, as we observe a wide variety of economic successes in radically different cultures. Nor can it be explained by lack of entrepreneurial spirit, as entrepreneurship is robust in every major city in the developing world. Instead, de Soto believes that underdevelopment is best explained by the lack of legal recognition of property rights. The lack of documentation means that people cannot readily turn their possessions into capital. Their capital is "dead": only exchangeable within a narrow circle and unusable in the broader world as collateral. The obvious solution to dead capital is to breathe life back into it through legally documenting ownership. Formalizing and documenting informal property claims allow individuals to develop a credit history and provides them an address for collection of debt and taxes, which forms the basis for the state to create reliable and universal public utilities.

The argument is as eloquent as it is obvious, but obvious and eloquent arguments are not always true, at least not in every context. Much evidence supports it, and legal titling has been shown to improve investment, both public and private, in countries such as Peru (Field 2005, 2007) and Argentina (Di Tella, Galiani, and Schargrodsky 2007; Galiani and Schargrodsky 2010). But much other evidence questions the benefits of legal titling, even in Peru (Kerekes and Williamson 2008, 2010) and Argentina (Altrichter and Basurto 2008). Because the argument in favor of legal titling is straightforward, we focus our discussion on potential problems that can result in lackluster results if not outright failure.

One place where titling appears to function relatively poorly is sub-Saharan Africa (see Atwood 1990; Bassett, Blanc-Pamard, and Boutrais 2007; Coldham 1979; Hunt 2004; Jacoby and Minten 2007; Leeson and Harris 2018b; Migot-Adholla et al. 1994). Part of the explanation is that colonial efforts at titling and encouraging development aimed to replace traditional property structures rather than to recognize and develop the existing ones. Legal titles with state backing were often at odds with historical and customary claims to land and were often part of a selective-enforcement regime. In many instances, the colonial effort to reduce the complex indigenous institutions to simple legal titles administered through a centralized legal process (Lund 2008) resulted in further insecurity because rather than fully replacing the existing property institutions, it simply weakened customary governance and holdings and achieved ambiguous results (Brasselle, Gaspart, and Platteau 2002; Bromley 2009b).

Another part of the challenge of titling in the region stems from the presumption of policy makers (both international and domestic) that those who have informal tenures suffer land-tenure insecurity when, in reality, they may have secure ownership (Sjaastad and Bromley 1997, 2000). This is the argument that Williamson and Kerekes (2011) make in explaining the lackluster results of titling in Peru: The informal arrangement provided a powerful foundation for secure rights, and extending the power of the relatively predatory state only served to undermine property security. In other words, throughout much of the world, state interference is the source of property insecurity rather than the solution to it (Alden Wily 2011).

Like the emergence of property rights more generally, the success of legal titling depends heavily on features of politics (Murtazashvili and Murtazashvili

2019), including the state's capacity to change the law and the basic administrative ability to provide a registry of landownership (Arruñada 2014). Such capacity is especially lacking in weak states, which is why a more logical sequence in such contexts would be to focus on establishing state administrative capacity before initiating land registration through a legal process (I. Murtazashvili and Murtazashvili 2016b). Successful legal titling also requires binding political constraints. Because legal titling involves the creation of property rights, the inability of the state to credibly commit to not expropriating landowners may be an issue. In addition, to ensure the property institutions work well, institutions such as polycentrism, which allows for experimentation, knowledge generation, and proper incentives through competition (Tiebout 1956), are likely to improve the quality of property rights by encouraging marginal improvements in their design and that they are a fit with the demands of those seeking legal property rights.

These studies emphasize that the success of legal titling often depends on the quality of governance in the places it is implemented (Deininger and Feder 2009). Many others also demonstrate that in many contexts, land is not valuable enough to justify the often-substantial costs of registering ownership (Platteau 2000) or that deliberate institutional ambiguity can serve an important economic function, such as enabling flexible responses to government predation or ineffective regulations (Ho 2001, 2014, 2016; Holland 2017). To the extent that some of the cases can be considered marginally successful, it is usually only a small subset of the population that gains in a selective-enforcement regime. In particular, it is very common for women to be excluded from the process and gains of legal titling (Joireman 2008; Tripp 1997, 2004). Accordingly, institutional representation of women, including quotas, is associated with greater protection of property rights (Brulé 2020). Beyond these issues, formalization can help further the political conflicts mentioned in Section 3. y of these ideas apply equally to housing, much of which is not formally approved by the relevant government. One solution is to legally recognize informal housing, though informality in rights to housing may allow for flexible and temporary rights. Sun and Ho (2018) suggest that informal housing serves an important economic function in China for low-income people such as migrant workers. Efforts to create legal rights to such housing may undermine such flexibility.

Related to land titling is the question of what to do with people who have been displaced by war. Some of the challenges involve competing claims to land that may arise from lack of registration before conflict or that records have been destroyed in conflict. Those occupying lands may be seeking to escape vulnerability. Hence, resolving a conflict by returning land to the original owners may create new vulnerabilities. The challenge of returnees suggests the need for clarification of legal ownership, though the nature of such conflicts strongly suggests that what is critical is an inclusive process that allows for competing claimants to participate in the process of sorting out ownership.

5.3 Land Grabbing

Another challenge in land policy is land grabbing, which is sometimes defined as efforts by powerful countries to acquire land to feed their populations. It is especially used to describe large industrializing countries, such as Brazil (Borras Jr. et al. 2011), and when the government-acquired land is used for growing domestic populations (Hall et al. 2015). Thus, land grabbing can be conceptualized as efforts by the state to serve political purposes by acquiring through political power land that is claimed by others. In Latin America, for example, land grabbing means government acquisition of land without respect for indigenous and cultural rights (Borras Jr. et al. 2012).

Large-scale market purchases of land, including purchases by governments, are not an economic problem and do not constitute land grabs. For example, China owns much land in the United States – by some estimates, an amount equal to the size of Vermont. The issue of land grabbing arises when governments use coercive powers to acquire land from one group and give it to another, which is a specific example of selective enforcement, as discussed in Section 2. In other cases of selective enforcement, the rents extracted by a domestic government are shared with outside governments.

An important part of the solution to land grabbing is political and institutional reform. Legal titling is not enough. Simply presenting the government with a title is not enough to prevent it from allocating land to benefit political decision makers, bureaucrats, or other groups. Rather, collective action to limit the grabbing hands of the state is necessary.

5.4 Technology to the Rescue?

As Yandle and Morriss (2001: 125) argue, "Technologies that reduce transaction costs allow individuals to engage in increased wealth-increasing trades. When such technologies allow the creation of private property rights, entrepreneurs facilitate the creation of new bundles of property rights to meet the demand for property ... Technology, either in law or in a more conventional sense, allows increasingly sophisticated definitions of property rights." One emerging technology that might provide a solution to the high-transaction-cost world of government registration and legal titling is blockchain.

Blockchain is a trustless distributed network technology that allows exchanges to be entered onto a ledger without requiring a third party to verify the entries (Davidson, De Filippi, and Potts 2018). One potential technological solution to the issue of a regime characterized by selective registration and enforcement is to implement blockchain technology to record who owns land in ways that cannot be manipulated. As Buchanan (1975) argues, one of the key productive functions of a state is to record information – data on people, land, and other things. Blockchain can provide a low-cost and secure way to fulfill this productive function.

However, lowering the cost of registration does little to provide security if the predatory state with disproportionate coercive power wishes to expropriate one's land – ledgers be damned. As long as the state enforces the rights, the pesky fundamental political dilemma presents itself. So blockchain is not perfect. Still, other technological innovations could be implemented alongside blockchain to reduce transaction costs even more. Yandle and Morriss (2001), for example, consider legal technologies for enforcing property rights, including common law and statutory law. With the right legal technology, combined with both traditional and emerging technologies (for example, barbed-wire fencing and blockchain), a robust property regime that avoids predation and allows for wealth creation may be more feasible where it currently is lacking.

6. Conclusion

At the forefront of the institutional renaissance are the Austrians, public choice theorists, and new institutionalists – those "who sit in the seat of Adam Smith."[35] Yet the observant reader will have noticed that the citations throughout this book extend far beyond Mises and Hayek, Buchanan and Tullock, and North and Ostrom. Nevertheless, it is the insights offered by these scholars and their associated schools of thought that are, in our view, necessary to understand both the origins and consequences of property rights.

Without the Austrian emphasis on spontaneous orders and its differentiation between cosmos and taxis, it would not be possible to fully understand the distinction between divergent origins of economic and legal property rights. And without this distinction, it would be difficult to understand failed reform and lackluster legal titles throughout the developing world. Limiting the investigation to the rules on the books, those created and enforced by states, severely hinders our ability to understand the development and wealth of nations. The Austrian focus on information and knowledge also provides a key insight as to why attempts to design a functioning system of property, let alone a whole functioning social order, tend toward failure.

---

[35] This phrase comes from a quote by Lord Acton and is used by Boettke (2012) to encompass the "mainline" of economics.

So does the public choice school's insight and their consistent application of incentives arising from political decision makers having more power than others in society. According to the Fragile States Index, more than half the governments in the world are weak or failed states.[36] The old model of a benevolent, omniscient, and dictatorial state that public choice theorists fought against prevented any understanding of real-world governance (Aligica, Boettke, and Tarko 2019). Even if we knew the proper rules for wealth creation in all contexts, the existing state, with its existing incentives, might not get us there. It would be better and more realistic to start from an assumption of anarchy (Rajan 2004). The public choice emphasis on incentive alignment encourages us to focus on when and where failure or success might occur. It helps us, for example, understand why selective enforcement results in stagnation in most instances but can align incentives in an unstable system. Given the importance of the state, both for good and for bad, in determining the form and function of a property rights system, it is necessary to remove the romance from politics (Buchanan 1984) and analytically investigate why states fail or succeed.

And without new institutionalism, particularly that of the Bloomington School and their focus on institutional diversity, the nuances associated with a functioning property rights system would be absent from the foreground of analysis. Context matters. Details matter. Constraints, values, and opportunity costs matter. Given the difficulty of centrally planning a social order (Austrian emphasis) and the potential for misaligned incentives when centrally creating and enforcing the institutional structure (public choice emphasis), decentralized experimentation and polycentricity are a necessary part of discovering what works (Bloomington emphasis). The naïve one-size-fits-all model of property in which everything must be owned either privately by individuals or by the state leads the analysis of property rights astray (Bromley 2019). Institutionalism brings back the focus to the ability – and the conditions that affect this ability – to create and enforce a system of property rights.

Whatever its origins – spontaneous or designed, state or extralegal, private or not – if a property rights system is to have beneficial consequences, it needs to reflect, in evolution or design, the existing constraints. And this can only occur when incentives are aligned and knowledge of relative prices can be generated and gathered. To understand whether this occurs, and hence to understand the nature and causes of the wealth of nations, Austrian, public choice, and new institutionalist insights are not simply useful conveniences, but necessities.

---

[36] https://fragilestatesindex.org/data

References

Acemoglu, Daron. 2003. "Why Not a Political Coase Theorem? Social Conflict, Commitment, and Politics." *Journal of Comparative Economics* 31(4): 620–52.

Acemoglu, Daron, and Simon Johnson. 2005. "Unbundling Institutions." *Journal of Political Economy* 113(5): 949–95.

Acemoglu, Daron, Simon Johnson, and James A. Robinson. 2003. "An African Success Story: Botswana." In *In Search of Prosperity: Analytic Narratives on Economic Growth*, ed. Dani Rodrik. Princeton: Princeton University Press, 80–122.

2005. "Institutions as a Fundamental Cause of Long-Run Growth." In *Handbook of Economic Growth*, eds. Philippe Aghion and Steven N. Durlauf. Amsterdam: North-Holland, 385–472.

Acemoglu, Daron, Tristan Reed, and James A. Robinson. 2014. "Chiefs: Economic Development and Elite Control of Civil Society in Sierra Leone." *Journal of Political Economy* 122(2): 319–68.

Acemoglu, Daron, and James A. Robinson. 2002. "The Political Economy of the Kuznets Curve." *Review of Development Economics* 6(2): 183–203.

2012. *Why Nations Fail: The Origins of Power, Prosperity, and Poverty.* New York: Crown Business.

2019. *The Narrow Corridor: States, Societies, and the Fate of Liberty.* New York: Penguin Press.

Agrawal, Arun, and Clark C. Gibson. 1999. "Enchantment and Disenchantment: The Role of Community in Natural Resource Conservation." *World Development* 27(4): 629–49.

Albertus, Michael, and Oliver Kaplan. 2013. "Land Reform as a Counterinsurgency Policy: Evidence from Colombia." *Journal of Conflict Resolution* 57(2): 198–231.

Alchian, Armen A. 1965. "Some Economics of Property Rights." *Il Politico*: 816–29.

Alchian, Armen A., and Harold Demsetz. 1972. "Production, Information Costs, and Economic Organization." *American Economic Review* 62(5): 777–95.

Alden Wily, Liz. 2011. "'The Law Is to Blame': The Vulnerable Status of Common Property Rights in Sub-Saharan Africa." *Development and Change* 42(3): 733–57.

Aldy, Joseph E., Scott Barrett, and Robert N. Stavins. 2003. "Thirteen Plus One: A Comparison of Global Climate Policy Architectures." *Climate Policy* 3 (4): 373–97.

Aligica, Paul Dragos. 2018. *Public Entrepreneurship, Citizenship, and Self-Governance*. New York: Cambridge University Press.

Aligica, Paul Dragos, Peter J. Boettke, and Vlad Tarko. 2019. *Public Governance and the Classical-Liberal Perspective: Political Economy Foundations*. New York: Oxford University Press.

Allen, Darcy W. E., and Jason Potts. 2016. "How Innovation Commons Contribute to Discovering and Developing New Technologies." *International Journal of the Commons* 10(2): 1035–54.

Allen, Douglas W. 1991a. "Homesteading and Property Rights; Or, 'How the West Was Really Won.'" *Journal of Law and Economics* 34(1): 1–23.

   1991b. "What Are Transaction Costs." *Research in Law and Economics* 14 (1): 1–18.

   2015. "The Coase Theorem: Coherent, Logical, and Not Disproved." *Journal of Institutional Economics* 11(2): 379–90.

   2019. "Establishing Economic Property Rights by Giving Away an Empire." *Journal of Law and Economics* 62(2): 251–80.

Allen, Douglas W., and Bryan Leonard. 2020. "Rationing by Racing and the Oklahoma Land Rushes." *Journal of Institutional Economics* 16(2): 127–44.

Alston, Eric, Lee J. Alston, Bernardo Mueller, and Tomas Nonnenmacher. 2018. *Institutional and Organizational Analysis: Concepts and Applications*. Cambridge University Press.

Alston, Lee J. 2017. "Beyond Institutions: Beliefs and Leadership." *The Journal of Economic History* 77(2): 353–72.

Alston, Lee J., Gary D. Libecap, and Bernardo Mueller. 1999. *Titles, Conflict, and Land Use: The Development of Property Rights and Land Reform on the Brazilian Amazon Frontier*. Ann Arbor: University of Michigan Press.

Alston, Lee J., Marcus André Melo, Bernardo Mueller, and Carlos Pereira. 2016. *Brazil in Transition: Beliefs, Leadership, and Institutional Change*. Princeton: Princeton University Press.

Altrichter, Mariana, and Xavier Basurto. 2008. "Effects of Land Privatisation on the Use of Common-Pool Resources of Varying Mobility in the Argentine Chaco." *Conservation and Society* 6(2): 154.

Anderson, Perry. 1974. *Passages from Antiquity to Feudalism*. London: New Left Books.

Anderson, Terry L., and Peter J. Hill. 1975. "The Evolution of Property Rights: A Study of the American West." *The Journal of Law and Economics* 18(1): 163–79.

1983. "Privatizing the Commons: An Improvement?" *Southern Economic Journal* 50(2): 438–50.

1990. "The Race for Property Rights." *Journal of Law and Economics* 33(1): 177–97.

eds. 2001. *The Technology of Property Rights*. Boston: Rowman & Littlefield.

2004. *The Not So Wild, Wild West: Property Rights on the Frontier*. Palo Alto: Stanford University Press.

Anderson, Terry L., and Bryan Leonard. 2016. "Institutions and the Wealth of Indian Nations." In *Unlocking the Wealth of Indian Nations*, ed. Terry L. Anderson. Palo Alto: Stanford University Press, 3–17.

Anderson, Terry L., and Gary D. Libecap. 2014. *Environmental Markets: A Property Rights Approach*. New York: Cambridge University Press.

Anderson, Terry L., and Dean Lueck. 1992. "Land Tenure and Agricultural Productivity on Indian Reservations." *The Journal of Law and Economics* 35(2): 427–54.

Anderson, Terry L., and Fred S. McChesney. 1994. "Raid or Trade? An Economic Model of Indian-White Relations." *Journal of Law and Economics* 37(1): 39–74.

Anderson, Terry L., and Dominic P. Parker. 2008. "Sovereignty, Credible Commitments, and Economic Prosperity on American Indian Reservations." *The Journal of Law and Economics* 51(4): 641–66.

Arruñada, Benito. 2014. "Registries." *Man and the Economy* 1(2): 209–30.

Arslantaş, Yasin, Antoine Pietri, and Mehrdad Vahabi. 2019. "State Predation in Historical Perspective: The Case of Ottoman Müsadere Practice during 1695–1839." *Public Choice* 182(3–4): 417–42.

Atwood, David A. 1990. "Land Registration in Africa: The Impact on Agricultural Production." *World Development* 18(5): 659–71.

Baland, Jean-Marie, and James A. Robinson. 2012. "The Political Value of Land: Political Reform and Land Prices in Chile." *American Journal of Political Science* 56(3): 601–19.

Bardhan, Pranab. 1973. "Size, Productivity, and Returns to Scale: An Analysis of Farm-Level Data in Indian Agriculture." *Journal of Political Economy* 81(6): 1370–86.

Barrett, Scott. 2010. *Why Cooperate? The Incentive to Supply Global Public Goods*. New York: Oxford University Press.

Barrett, Scott, and Robert Stavins. 2003. "Increasing Participation and Compliance in International Climate Change Agreements." *International Environmental Agreements* 3(4): 349–76.

Barzel, Yoram. 1997. *Economic Analysis of Property Rights*. New York: Cambridge University Press.

2002. *A Theory of the State: Economic Rights, Legal Rights, and the Scope of the State*. New York: Cambridge University Press.

Bassett, Thomas J., Chantal Blanc-Pamard, and Jean Boutrais. 2007. "Constructing Locality: The Terroir Approach in West Africa." *Africa* 77 (1): 104–29.

Bates, Robert H. 1981. *Markets and States in Tropical Africa: The Political Basis of Agricultural Policies*. Berkeley: University of California Press.

2017. *The Development Dilemma: Security, Prosperity, and a Return to History*. Princeton: Princeton University Press.

Belloc, Marianna, and Samuel Bowles. 2013. "The Persistence of Inferior Cultural-Institutional Conventions." *American Economic Review* 103(3): 93–98.

2017. "Persistence and Change in Culture and Institutions under Autarchy, Trade, and Factor Mobility." *American Economic Journal: Microeconomics* 9(4): 245–76.

Benjaminsen, Tor A., Stein Holden, Christian Lund, and Espen Sjaastad. 2009. "Formalisation of Land Rights: Some Empirical Evidence from Mali, Niger and South Africa." *Land Use Policy* 26(1): 28–35.

Benson, Bruce L. 1989a. "Enforcement of Private Property Rights in Primitive Societies: Law without Government." *Journal of Libertarian Studies* 9(1): 1–26.

1989b. "The Spontaneous Evolution of Commercial Law." *Southern Economic Journal* 55(3): 644–61.

2006. "Property Rights and the Buffalo Economy of the Great Plains." In *Self-Determination: The Other Path for Native Americans*, eds. Terry L. Anderson, Bruce L. Benson, and Thomas Flanagan. Palo Alto: Stanford University Press, 29–67.

Block, Walter E., and Peter L. Nelson. 2015. *Water Capitalism: The Case for Privatizing Oceans, Rivers, Lakes, and Aquifers*. Lanham, MD: Lexington Books.

Boettke, Peter J. 1989. "Evolution and Economics: Austrians as Institutionalists." *Research in the History of Economic Thought and Methodology* 6: 73–89.

2001. *Calculation and Coordination: Essays on Socialism and Transitional Political Economy*. New York: Routledge.

2012. *Living Economics*. Oakland, CA: The Independent Institute.

Boettke, Peter J., and Rosolino Candela. 2020. "Productive Specialization, Peaceful Cooperation, and the Problem of the Predatory State: Lessons from Comparative Historical Political Economy." *Public Choice* 182 (3–4): 331–52.

Boettke, Peter J., and Christopher J. Coyne. 2005. "Methodological Individualism, Spontaneous Order and the Research Program of the Workshop in Political Theory and Policy Analysis." *Journal of Economic Behavior & Organization* 57(2): 145–58.

Boettke, Peter J., Christopher J. Coyne, and Peter T. Leeson. 2011. "Quasimarket Failure." *Public Choice* 149(1–2): 209–24.

2013. "Comparative Historical Political Economy." *Journal of Institutional Economics* 9(3): 285–301.

Boettke, Peter J., Christopher J. Coyne, and Patrick Newman. 2016. "The History of a Tradition: Austrian Economics from 1871 to 2016." In *Research in the History of Economic Thought and Methodology*, Emerald Group Publishing Limited, 199–243.

Bonney, Richard. 1999. *The Rise of the Fiscal State in Europe c. 1200–1815*. New York: Oxford University Press.

Boone, Catherine. 2009. "Electoral Populism Where Property Rights Are Weak: Land Politics in Contemporary Sub-Saharan Africa." *Comparative Politics*: 183–201.

2013. *Property and Political Order in Africa: Land Rights and the Structure of Politics*. New York: Cambridge University Press.

Borras Jr, Saturnino M. et al. 2011. "Towards a Better Understanding of Global Land Grabbing: An Editorial Introduction." *The Journal of Peasant Studies* 38(2): 209–16.

2012. "Land Grabbing in Latin America and the Caribbean." *The Journal of Peasant Studies* 39(3–4): 845–72.

Brasselle, Anne-Sophie, Frederic Gaspart, and Jean-Philippe Platteau. 2002. "Land Tenure Security and Investment Incentives: Puzzling Evidence from Burkina Faso." *Journal of Development Economics* 67(2): 373–418.

Brennan, Geoffrey, and James M. Buchanan. 1985. *The Reason of Rules: Constitutional Political Economy*. New York: Cambridge University Press.

Brewer, John. 1990. *The Sinews of Power: War, Money, and the English State, 1688–1783*. Cambridge: Harvard University Press.

Bromley, Daniel W. 1991. *Environment and Economy: Property Rights and Public Policy*. Oxford: Blackwell Publishers.

2006. *Sufficient Reason: Volitional Pragmatism and the Meaning of Economic Institutions*. Princeton: Princeton University Press.

2008. "The Crisis in Ocean Governance: Conceptual Confusion, Spurious Economics, Political Indifference." *MAST: Maritime Studies* 6(2): 7–22.

2009a. "Abdicating Responsibility: The Deceits of Fisheries Policy." *Fisheries* 34(6): 280–90.

2009b. "Formalising Property Relations in the Developing World: The Wrong Prescription for the Wrong Malady." *Land Use Policy* 26(1): 20–27.

2019. *Possessive Individualism: A Crisis of Capitalism*. New York: Oxford University Press.

Brulé, Rachel E. 2020. *Women, Power,* and Property: The Paradox of Gender Equality Laws in India. Cambridge University Press.

Buchanan, James M. 1949. "The Pure Theory of Government Finance: A Suggested Approach." *Journal of Political Economy* 57(6): 496–505.

1965. "An Economic Theory of Clubs." *Economica* 32(125): 1–14.

1975. *The Limits of Liberty: Between Anarchy and Leviathan*. Chicago: University of Chicago Press.

1984. "Politics without Romance: A Sketch of Positive Public Choice Theory and Its Normative Implications." In *The Theory of Public Choice II*, eds. James M. Buchanan and Robert D. Tollison. Ann Arbor: University of Michigan Press, 11–22.

1986. *Liberty, Market and State: Political Economy in the 1980s*. Brighton: Wheatsheaf Books.

Bustamante, Pedro, Marcela M. Gomez, Ilia Murtazashvili, and Martin BH Weiss. 2020. "Spectrum Anarchy: Why Self-Governance of the Radio Spectrum Works Better than We Think." *Journal of Institutional Economics*. https://www.cambridge.org/core/journals/journal-of-institutional-econom ics/article/spectrum-anarchy-why-selfgovernance-of-the-radio-spectrum-works-better-than-we-think/52ADD1233BA84EC49F7B3882FD8B5971

Buxton, Carol R. 2004. "Property in Outer Space: The Common Heritage of Mankind Principle vs. the First in Time, First in Right, Rule of Property." *Journal of Air Law and Commerce* 69(4): 689–707.

Cai, Meina, Pengfei Liu, and Hui Wang. 2020. "Political Trust, Risk Preferences, and Policy Support: A Study of Land-Dispossessed Villagers in China." *World Development* 125: 104687.

Cai, Meina, Ilia Murtazashvili, Jennifer Brick Murtazashvili, and Hui Wang. (forthcoming). "Sugarcoating the Bitter Pill: Compensation, Land

Governance, and Opposition to Land Expropriation in China." *Journal* of Peasant Studies. http://doi. 10.1080/03066150.2020.1824180

Cai, Meina, Ilia Murtazashvili, Jennifer Murtazashvili, and Raufhon Salahodjaev. 2020. "Individualism and Governance of the Commons." *Public Choice* 184(1–2): 175–95.

Cai, Meina, Jennifer Murtazashvili, and Ilia Murtazashvili. 2020. "The Politics of Land Property Rights." *Journal of Institutional Economics* 12(2): 151–67.

Calvert, Randall. 1995. "The Rational Choice Theory of Social Institutions: Cooperation, Coordination, and Communication." In *Modern Political Economy: Old Topics, New Directions*, eds. Jeffrey S. Banks and Eric A. Hanushek. New York: Cambridge University Press, 216–68.

Candela, Rosolino A. 2020. "The Political Economy of Insecure Property Rights: Insights from the Kingdom of Sicily." *Journal of Institutional Economics* 16(2): 233–49.

Candela, Rosolino A., and Vincent J. Geloso. 2018. "The Lightship in Economics." *Public Choice* 176(3–4): 479–506.

Carlson, Leonard A. 1981. "Land Allotment and the Decline of American Indian Farming." *Explorations in Economic History* 18(2): 128.

Carugati, Federica. 2019. *Creating a Constitution: Law, Democracy, and Growth in Ancient Athens*. Princeton: Princeton University Press.

Carugati, Federica, Josiah Ober, and Barry R. Weingast. 2019. "Is Development Uniquely Modern? Ancient Athens on the Doorstep." *Public Choice* 181 (1–2): 29–47.

Castillo, Juan Camilo, Daniel Mejía, and Pascual Restrepo. 2020. "Scarcity without Leviathan: The Violent Effects of Cocaine Supply Shortages in the Mexican Drug War." *Review of Economics and Statistics* 102(2): 269–86.

Cheung, Steven N. S. 1969. *The Theory of Share Tenancy: With Special Application to Asian Agriculture and the First Phase of Taiwan Land Reform*. Chicago: University of Chicago Press.

Cheung, Steven N.S. 1970. "The Structure of a Contract and the Theory of a Non-Exclusive Resource." *Journal of Law and Economics*: 49–70.

Chhatre, Ashwini, and Arun Agrawal. 2008. "Forest Commons and Local Enforcement." *Proceedings of the National Academy of Sciences* 105 (36): 13286–91.

Choumert, Johanna, Pascale Combes Motel, and Hervé K. Dakpo. 2013. "Is the Environmental Kuznets Curve for Deforestation a Threatened Theory? A Meta-Analysis of the Literature." *Ecological Economics* 90: 19–28.

Clark, J. R., and Benjamin Powell. 2019. "The 'Minimal' State Reconsidered: Governance on the Margin." *The Review of Austrian Economics* 32(2): 119–30.

Clay, Karen. 1999. "Property Rights and Institutions: Congress and the California Land Act 1851." *Journal of Economic History* 59(01): 122–42.

Clay, Karen, and Gavin Wright. 2005. "Order without Law? Property Rights during the California Gold Rush." *Explorations in Economic History* 42 (2): 155–83.

Coase, Ronald H. 1960. "The Problem of Social Cost." *Journal of Law and Economics* 3: 1–44.

2013. "The Federal Communications Commission." *Journal of Law and Economics* 56(4): 879–915.

Coldham, Simon FR. 1979. "Land-Tenure Reform in Kenya: The Limits of Law." *The Journal of Modern African Studies* 17(4): 615–27.

Cole, Daniel H., Graham Epstein, and Michael D. McGinnis. 2014. "Digging Deeper into Hardin's Pasture: The Complex Institutional Structure of 'The Tragedy of the Commons.'" *Journal of Institutional Economics* 10(3): 353–69.

2019. "Combining the IAD and SES Frameworks." *International Journal of the Commons* 13(1): 244–75.

Conning, Jonathan H., and James A. Robinson. 2007. "Property Rights and the Political Organization of Agriculture." *Journal of Development Economics* 82(2): 416–47.

Cornell, Stephen, and Joseph P. Kalt. 1998. "Sovereignty and Nation-Building: The Development Challenge in Indian Country Today." *American Indian Culture and Research Journal* 22(3): 187–214.

2000. "Where's the Glue? Institutional and Cultural Foundations of American Indian Economic Development." *The Journal of Socio-Economics* 29(5): 443–70.

Costello, Christopher, Steven D. Gaines, and John Lynham. 2008. "Can Catch Shares Prevent Fisheries Collapse?" *Science* 321(5896): 1678–81.

Cowen, Nick, and Charles Delmotte. 2021. "Ostrom, Floods and Mismatched Property Rights." *International Journal of the Commons*.

Cowen, Tyler. 1992. "Law as a Public Good: The Economics of Anarchy." *Economics & Philosophy* 8(2): 249–67.

Cox, Michael, Gwen Arnold, and Sergio Villamayor Tomás. 2010. "*A Review of Design Principles for Community-Based Natural Resource Management.*" In Elinor Ostrom and the Bloomington School of Political Economy: Resource Governance, eds. Daniel H. Cole and Michael D. McGinnis. Lanham, MD: Lexington Books.

Crepelle, Adam, and Ilia Murtazashvili. 2020. "COVID-19, Indian Reservations, and Self-Determination." Mercatus COVID-19 Response Policy Brief.

Davidson, Sinclair, Primavera De Filippi, and Jason Potts. 2018. "Blockchains and the Economic Institutions of Capitalism." *Journal of Institutional Economics* 14(4): 639–58.

De Long, J. Bradford, and Andrei Shleifer. 1993. "Princes and Merchants: European City Growth before the Industrial Revolution." *The Journal of Law and Economics* 36(2): 671–702.

Deakin, Simon, et al. 2017. "Legal Institutionalism: Capitalism and the Constitutive Role of Law." *Journal of Comparative Economics* 45(1): 188–200.

Deal, Robert. 2016. *The Law of the Whale Hunt: Dispute Resolution, Property Law, and American Whalers, 1780–1880*. New York: Cambridge University Press.

Deininger, Klaus, and Gershon Feder. 2009. "Land Registration, Governance, and Development: Evidence and Implications for Policy." *The World Bank Research Observer* 24(2): 233–66.

Demsetz, Harold. 1967. "Toward a Theory of Property Rights." *American Economic Review* 57(2): 347–59.

1969. "Information and Efficiency: Another Viewpoint." *Journal of Law and Economics* 12(1): 1–22.

Denzau, Arthur T., and Douglass C. North. 1994. "Shared Mental Models: Ideologies and Institutions." *Kyklos* 47(1): 3–31.

Di Tella, Rafael, Sebastian Galiani, and Ernesto Schargrodsky. 2007. "The Formation of Beliefs: Evidence from the Allocation of Land Titles to Squatters." *The Quarterly Journal of Economics*: 209–41.

Dickson, Bruce J. 2003. *Red Capitalists in China: The Party, Private Entrepreneurs, and Prospects for Political Change*. New York: Cambridge University Press.

2008. *Wealth into Power: The Communist Party's Embrace of China's Private Sector*. New York: Cambridge University Press.

Diermeier, Daniel, Joel M. Ericson, Timothy Frye, and Steve Lewis. 1997. "Credible Commitment and Property Rights: The Role of Strategic Interaction between Political and Economic Actors." In *The Political Economy of Property Rights*: 20–42.

Dikötter, Frank. 2010. *Mao's Great Famine: The History of China's Most Devastating Catastrophe, 1958–1962*. Bloomsbury Publishing US.

Dincecco, Mark. 2011. *Political Transformations and Public Finances: Europe, 1650–1913*. New York: Cambridge University Press.

Dincecco, Mark, and Massimiliano Gaetano Onorato. 2017. *From Warfare to Wealth*. New York: Cambridge University Press.

Dippel, Christian, and Dustin Frye. 2019. *The Effect of Land Allotment on Native American Households during the Assimilation Era*. Technical report, Working Paper.

Dourado, Eli, and Alex Tabarrok. 2015. "Public Choice Perspectives on Intellectual Property." *Public Choice* 163(1–2): 129–51.

Dutta, Nabamita, Peter T. Leeson, and Claudia R. Williamson. 2013. "The Amplification Effect: Foreign Aid's Impact on Political Institutions." *Kyklos* 66(2): 208–28.

Eggertsson, Thrainn. 1990. *Economic Behavior and Institutions: Principles of Neoinstitutional Economics*. New York: Cambridge University Press.

Ellickson, Robert C. 1991. *Order without Law: How Neighbors Settle Disputes*. Cambridge: Harvard University Press.

Ely Jr, James W. 2007. *The Guardian of Every Other Right: A Constitutional History of Property Rights*. New York: Oxford University Press.

Ferrell, Perry. 2019. "Titles for Me but Not for Thee: Transitional Gains Trap of Property Rights Extension in Colombia." *Public Choice* 178(1): 95–114.

Field, Barry C. 1989. "The Evolution of Property Rights." *Kyklos* 42(3): 319–45.

Field, Erica. 2005. "Property Rights and Investment in Urban Slums." *Journal of the European Economic Association* 3(2-3): 279–90.

2007. "Entitled to Work: Urban Property Rights and Labor Supply in Peru." *The Quarterly Journal of Economics* 122(4): 1561–1602.

Fogel, Robert W., and Stanley L. Engerman. 1974. *Time on the Cross: The Economics of American Negro Slavery*. Boston: Little, Brown and Company.

Foner, Eric. 1971. *Free Soil, Free Labor, Free Men: The Ideology of the Republican Party before the Civil War*. New York: Oxford University Press.

Foss, Nicolai J. 1997. "On Austrian and Neo-Institutionalist Economics." In *Austrian Economics in Debate*, eds. Willem Keizer, Bert Teiben, and Rudy van Zijp. London and New York: Routledge, 243.

Friedman, David. 1979. "Private Creation and Enforcement of Law: A Historical Case." *The Journal of Legal Studies* 8(2): 399–415.

Friedman, David D. 2005. "From Imperial China to Cyberspace: Contracting without the State." *Journal of Law, Economics & Policy* 1: 349–70.

Frischmann, Brett M., Michael J. Madison, and Katherine Jo Strandburg. 2014. *Governing Knowledge Commons*. New York: Oxford University Press.

Frischmann, Brett M., Alain Marciano, and Giovanni Battista Ramello. 2019. "Retrospectives: Tragedy of the Commons after 50 Years." *Journal of Economic Perspectives* 33(4): 211–28.

Frye, Dustin. 2016. "Paternalism versus Sovereignty: The Long Run Economic Effects of the Indian Reorganization Act." In *Unlocking the Wealth of Indian Nations*, ed. Terry L. Anderson. Lanham, MD: Lexington Books.

Furubotn, Eirik G., and Svetozar Pejovich. 1972. "Property Rights and Economic Theory: A Survey of Recent Literature." *Journal of Economic Literature* 10(4): 1137–62.

Galiani, Sebastian, and Ernesto Schargrodsky. 2010. "Property Rights for the Poor: Effects of Land Titling." *Journal of Public Economics* 94(9): 700–29.

Gehlbach, Scott, and Philip Keefer. 2011. "Investment without Democracy: Ruling-Party Institutionalization and Credible Commitment in Autocracies." *Journal of Comparative Economics* 39(2): 123–39.

Geloso, Vincent, and Jamie Bologna Pavlik. (forthcoming). "Economic Freedom and the Economic Consequences of the 1918 Pandemic." *Contemporary Economic Policy.* https://onlinelibrary.wiley.com/doi/full/10.1111/coep.12504

Geloso, Vincent J., and Alexander W. Salter. (2020). "State Capacity and Economic Development: Causal Mechanism or Correlative Filter?" *Journal of Economic Behavior & Organization* 170: 372–85. https://www.sciencedirect.com/science/article/abs/pii/S0167268119303981

Geloso, Vincent, and Ilia Murtazashvili. 2020. Can Governments Deal with Pandemics? SSRN. https://ssrn.com/abstract=3671634

Granovetter, Mark S. 1977. "The Strength of Weak Ties: A Network Theory Revisited." *Social Networks* 1: 201–33.

Grossman, Herschel I., and Minseong Kim. 1995. "Swords or Plowshares? A Theory of the Security of Claims to Property." *Journal of Political Economy*: 1275–88.

Grossman, Shelby. 2020. "The Politics of Order in Informal Markets: Evidence from Lagos." *World Politics.*

Guardado, Jenny. 2018. "Land Tenure, Price Shocks, and Insurgency: Evidence from Peru and Colombia." *World Development* 111: 256–69.

Haber, Stephen, Armando Razo, and Noel Maurer. 2003. *The Politics of Property Rights: Political Instability, Credible Commitments, and Economic Growth in Mexico, 1876–1929.* New York: Cambridge University Press.

Haddock, David D., and Lynne Kiesling. 2002. "The Black Death and Property Rights." *The Journal of Legal Studies* 31(S2): S545–87.

Hadfield, Gillian K. 2016. *Rules for a Flat World: Why Humans Invented Law and How to Reinvent It for a Complex Global Economy.* New York: Oxford University Press.

2017. "The Problem of Social Order: What Should We Count as Law?" *Law & Social Inquiry* 42(1): 16–27.

Hadfield, Gillian K., and Barry R. Weingast. 2014. "Microfoundations of the Rule of Law." *Annual Review of Political Science* 17: 21–42.

Hafer, Catherine. 2006. "On the Origins of Property Rights: Conflict and Production in the State of Nature." *The Review of Economic Studies* 73 (1): 119–43.

Hall, Ruth, et al. 2015. "Resistance, Acquiescence or Incorporation? An Introduction to Land Grabbing and Political Reactions 'from Below.'" *Journal of Peasant Studies* 42(3–4): 467–88.

Hardin, Garrett. 1968. "The Tragedy of the Commons." *Science* 162(3859): 1243–48.

Harris, Colin. 2018. "Institutional Solutions to Free-Riding in Peer-to-Peer Networks: A Case Study of Online Pirate Communities." *Journal of Institutional Economics* 14(5): 901–24.

Harris, Colin, and Adam Kaiser. (2020). "Burying the Hatchet." SSRN. https://ssrn.com/abstract=3701375

Hayek, F. A. 1945. "The Use of Knowledge in Society." *American Economic Review*: 519–30.

1973. *Law, Legislation and Liberty: A New Statement of the Liberal Principles of Justice and Political Economy.* Chicago: University Of Chicago Press.

1988. *The Fatal Conceit: The Errors of Socialism.* Chicago: University Of Chicago Press.

Hazlett, Thomas W. 2017. *The Political Spectrum: The Tumultuous Liberation of Wireless Technology, from Herbert Hoover to the Smartphone.* New Haven: Yale University Press.

Heilmann, Sebastian. 2008. "Policy Experimentation in China's Economic Rise." *Studies in Comparative International Development* 43(1): 1–26.

Heller, Michael A. 1998. "The Tragedy of the Anticommons: Property in the Transition from Marx to Markets." *Harvard Law Review*: 621–88.

Hendrickson, Joshua R., Alexander William Salter, and Brian C. Albrecht. 2018. "Preventing Plunder: Military Technology, Capital Accumulation, and Economic Growth." *Journal of Macroeconomics* 58: 154–73.

Heritier, Adrienne. 2007. *Explaining Institutional Change in Europe.* Oxford: Oxford University Press.

Hess, Charlotte, and Elinor Ostrom. 2007. *Understanding Knowledge as a Commons*. Cambridge: The MIT Press.

Heurlin, Christopher. 2016. *Responsive Authoritarianism in China*. New York: Cambridge University Press.

Hill, Peter J. 2014. "Are All Commons Tragedies? The Case of Bison in the Nineteenth Century." *The Independent Review* 18(4): 485–502.

Ho, Peter. 2001. "Who Owns China's Land? Policies, Property Rights and Deliberate Institutional Ambiguity." *The China Quarterly* 166: 394–421.

2005. *Institutions in Transition: Land Ownership, Property Rights and Social Conflict in China*. New York: Oxford University Press.

2014. "The 'Credibility Thesis' and Its Application to Property Rights: (In) Secure Land Tenure, Conflict and Social Welfare in China." *Land Use Policy* 40: 13–27.

2016. "An Endogenous Theory of Property Rights: Opening the Black Box of Institutions." *Journal of Peasant Studies* 43(6): 1121–44.

2017. *Unmaking China's Development: The Function and Credibility of Institutions*. New York: Cambridge University Press.

Hodgson, Geoffrey M. 1996. *Economics and Evolution: Bringing Life Back into Economics*. Ann Arbor: University of Michigan Press.

2002. *How Economics Forgot History: The Problem of Historical Specificity in Social Science*. London and New York: Routledge.

2007. "Evolutionary and Institutional Economics as the New Mainstream?" *Evolutionary and Institutional Economics Review* 4(1): 7–25.

2009. "On the Institutional Foundations of Law: The Insufficiency of Custom and Private Ordering." *Journal of Economic Issues* 43(1): 143–66.

2015a. *Conceptualizing Capitalism: Institutions, Evolution, Future*. Chicago: University of Chicago Press.

2015b. "Much of the 'Economics of Property Rights' Devalues Property and Legal Rights." *Journal of Institutional Economics* 11(4): 683–709.

2017. "1688 and All That: Property Rights, the Glorious Revolution and the Rise of British Capitalism." *Journal of Institutional Economics* 13(1): 79–107.

Holland, Alisha C. 2017. *Forbearance as Redistribution: The Politics of Informal Welfare in Latin America*. New York: Cambridge University Press.

Hoock, Holger. 2017. *Scars of Independence: America's Violent Birth*. New York: Crown.

Horowitz, Jeremy, and Kathleen Klaus. 2018. "Can Politicians Exploit Ethnic Grievances? An Experimental Study of Land Appeals in Kenya." *Political Behavior*: 1–24.

Hou, Yue. 2019. *The Private Sector in Public Office: Selective Property Rights in China*. New York: Cambridge University Press.

Hsing, You-tien. 2010. *The Great Urban Transformation: Politics of Land and Property in China*. New York: Oxford University Press.

Huang, Yasheng. 2008. *Capitalism with Chinese Characteristics: Entrepreneurship and the State*. Cambridge University Press.

Hummel, Jeffrey. 2013. *Emancipating Slaves, Enslaving Free Men: A History of the American Civil War*. Peru, IL: Open court.

Hunt, Diana. 2004. "Unintended Consequences of Land Rights Reform: The Case of the 1998 Uganda Land Act." *Development policy review* 22(2): 173–91.

Huntington, Samuel P. 1968. *Political Order in Changing Societies*. New Haven: Yale University Press.

Jacoby, Hanan G., and Bart Minten. 2007. "Is Land Titling in Sub-Saharan Africa Cost-Effective? Evidence from Madagascar." *The World Bank Economic Review* 21(3): 461–85.

Joireman, Sandra F. 2008. "The Mystery of Capital Formation in Sub-Saharan Africa: Women, Property Rights and Customary Law." *World Development* 36(7): 1233–46.

Kerekes, Carrie B., and Claudia R. Williamson. 2008. "Unveiling de Soto's Mystery: Property Rights, Capital Formation, and Development." *Journal of Institutional Economics* 4(3): 299.

2010. "Propertyless in Peru, Even with a Government Land Title." *American Journal of Economics and Sociology* 69(3): 1011–33.

2012. "Discovering Law: Hayekian Competition in Medieval Iceland." *Griffith Law Review* 21(2): 432–47.

Klaus, Kathleen. 2020. "Raising the Stakes: Land Titling and Electoral Stability in Kenya." *Journal of Peace Research* 57(1): 30–45.

2020. *Political Violence in Kenya: Land, Elections, and Claim-Making*. New York: Cambridge University Press.

Klaus, Kathleen, and Matthew I. Mitchell. 2015. "Land Grievances and the Mobilization of Electoral Violence: Evidence from Côte d'Ivoire and Kenya." *Journal of Peace Research* 52(5): 622–35.

Knight, Jack. 1992. *Institutions and Social Conflict*. New York: Cambridge University Press.

Knight, Jack, and Douglass C. North. 1997. "Explaining the Complexity of Institutional Change." In *The Political Economy of Property Rights:*

*Institutional Change and Credibility in the Reform of Centrally Planned Economies.*New York: Cambridge University Press, 349–54.

Knight, Jack, and Itai Sened, eds. 1995. *Explaining Social Institutions*. Ann Arbor: University of Michigan Press.

Kopsidis, Michael, and Daniel W. Bromley. 2016. "The French Revolution and German Industrialization: Dubious Models and Doubtful Causality." *Journal of Institutional Economics* 12(1): 161–90.

Kornai, Janos. 1992. *The Socialist System: The Political Economy of Communism*. New York: Oxford University Press.

Krueger, Anne O. 1974. "The Political Economy of the Rent-Seeking Society." *The American Economic Review* 64(3): 291–303.

Kuran, Timur. 2004. *Islam and Mammon: The Economic Predicaments of Islamism*. Princeton: Princeton University Press.

2011. *The Long Divergence: How Islamic Law Held Back the Middle East*. Princeton: Princeton University Press.

2020. "Zakat: Islam's Missed Opportunity to Limit Predatory Taxation." *Public Choice* 182(3–4): 395–416.

Kuznets, Simon. 1955. "Economic Growth and Income Inequality." *American Economic Review* 45(1): 1–28.

Leeson, Peter T. 2007a. "Anarchy, Monopoly, and Predation." *Journal of Institutional and Theoretical Economics* 163(3): 467–82.

2007b. "An-arrgh-chy: The Law and Economics of Pirate Organization." *Journal of political economy* 115(6): 1049–94.

2007c. "Better off Stateless: Somalia before and after Government Collapse." *Journal of Comparative Economics* 35(4): 689–710.

2007d. "Trading with Bandits." *The Journal of Law and Economics* 50(2): 303–21.

2008. "Coordination without Command: Stretching the Scope of Spontaneous Order." *Public Choice* 135(1–2): 67–78.

2009. "The Laws of Lawlessness." *The Journal of Legal Studies* 38(2): 471–503.

2010a. "Pirational Choice: The Economics of Infamous Pirate Practices." *Journal of Economic Behavior & Organization* 76(3): 497–510.

2010b. "Two Cheers for Capitalism?" *Society* 47(3): 227–33.

2011. *The Invisible Hook: The Hidden Economics of Pirates*. Princeton: Princeton University Press.

2014a. *Anarchy Unbound: Why Self-Governance Works Better than You Think*. New York: Cambridge University Press.

2014b. "Human Sacrifice." *Review of Behavioral Economics* 1(1–2): 137–65.

2020. "Logic Is a Harsh Mistress: Welfare Economics for Economists." *Journal of Institutional Economics* 16(2): 145–50.

Leeson, Peter T., and Colin Harris. 2018a. "Testing Rational Choice Theories of Institutional Change." *Rationality and Society* 30(4): 420–31.

2018b. "Wealth-Destroying Private Property Rights." *World Development* 107: 1–9.

Leeson, Peter T., Colin Harris, and Andrew Myers. 2020. "Kornai Goes to Kenya." *Public Choice*. https://link.springer.com/article/10.1007/s11127-020-00782-w

Leeson, Peter T., and Douglas B. Rogers. 2012. "Organizing Crime." *Supreme Court Economic Review* 20(1): 89–123.

Leeson, Peter T., and Paola A. Suarez. 2016. "An Economic Analysis of Magna Carta." *International Review of Law and Economics* 47: 40–46.

Leeson, Peter T., and Claudia R. Williamson. 2009. "Anarchy and Development: An Application of the Theory of Second Best." *The Law and Development Review* 2(1): 77–96.

Lemke, Jayme S. 2016. "Interjurisdictional Competition and the Married Women's Property Acts." *Public Choice* 166(3–4): 291–313.

Leonard, Bryan, Dominic Parker, and Terry Anderson. (forthcoming). "Land Quality, Land Rights, and Indigenous Poverty." *Journal of Development Economics*.

Lesorogol, Carolyn K. 2005. "Privatizing Pastoral Lands: Economic and Normative Outcomes in Kenya." *World Development* 33(11): 1959–78.

Levien, Michael. 2011. "Special Economic Zones and Accumulation by Dispossession in India." *Journal of Agrarian Change* 11(4): 454–83.

2012. "The Land Question: Special Economic Zones and the Political Economy of Dispossession in India." *The Journal of Peasant Studies* 39 (3–4): 933–69.

2018. *Dispossession without Development: Land Grabs in Neoliberal India.* New York: Oxford University Press.

Libecap, Gary D. 1989a. *Contracting for Property Rights.* New York: Cambridge University Press.

1989b. "Distributional Issues in Contracting for Property Rights." *Journal of Institutional and Theoretical Economics*: 6–24.

2005. "Chinatown: Owens Valley and Western Water Reallocation – Getting the Record Straight and What It Means for Water Markets." *Texas Law Review* 83(7): 2055–89.

2009. "Chinatown Revisited: Owens Valley and Los Angeles – Bargaining Costs and Fairness Perceptions of the First Major Water Rights Exchange." *Journal of Law, Economics, and organization* 25(2): 311–38.

2018. *Property Rights to Frontier Land and Minerals: US Exceptionalism.* National Bureau of Economic Research.

Libecap, Gary D., and Dean Lueck. 2011. "The Demarcation of Land and the Role of Coordinating Property Institutions." *Journal of Political Economy* 119(3): 426–67.

Libecap, Gary D., and James L. Smith. 1999. "The Self-Enforcing Provisions of Oil and Gas Unit Operating Agreements: Theory and Evidence." *Journal of Law, Economics, and Organization* 15(2): 526–48.

2002. "The Economic Evolution of Petroleum Property Rights in the United States." *The Journal of Legal Studies* 31(S2): S589–608.

Libecap, Gary D., and Steven N. Wiggins. 1985. "The Influence of Private Contractual Failure on Regulation: The Case of Oil Field Unitization." *Journal of Political Economy* 93(4): 690–714.

Liebowitz, Stan J., and Stephen E. Margolis. 1995. "Path Dependence, Lock-in, and History." *Journal of Law, Economics, & Organization* 11: 205.

Lin, Justin Yifu. 1992. "Rural Reforms and Agricultural Growth in China." *The American Economic Review*: 34–51.

Lipsey, Richard G., and Kelvin Lancaster. 1956. "The General Theory of Second Best." *The Review of Economic Studies* 24(1): 11–32.

Liu, Lizhi, and Barry R. Weingast. 2018. "Taobao, Federalism, and the Emergence of Law, Chinese Style." *Minnesota Law Review* 111: 1563–90.

Lueck, Dean. 1995. "The Rule of First Possession and the Design of the Law." *The Journal of Law and Economics* 38(2): 393–436.

2002. "The Extermination and Conservation of the American Bison." *The Journal of Legal Studies* 31(S2): S609–52.

Lund, Christian. 2008. *Local Politics and the Dynamics of Property in Africa.* New York: Cambridge University Press.

Macaulay, Stewart. 1963. "Non-Contractual Relations in Business: A Preliminary Study." *American Sociological Review* 28(1): 55–67.

Madison, Michael J., Brett M. Frischmann, and Katherine J. Strandburg. 2009. "Constructing Commons in the Cultural Environment." *Cornell Law Review* 95: 657.

Mailath, George J., and Larry Samuelson. 2006. *Repeated Games and Reputations: Long-Run Relationships.* New York: Oxford University Press.

Maskin, Eric, Yingyi Qian, and Chenggang Xu. 2000. "Incentives, Information, and Organizational Form." *Review of Economic Studies* 67(2): 359–78.

McChesney, Fred S. 1990. "Government as Definer of Property Rights: Indian Lands, Ethnic Externalities, and Bureaucratic Budgets." *Journal of Legal Studies*: 297–335.

McCloskey, Deirdre N. 2010. *Bourgeois Dignity: Why Economics Can't Explain the Modern World*. Chicago: University of Chicago Press.

   2016. "Max U versus Humanomics: A Critique of Neo-Institutionalism." *Journal of Institutional Economics* 12(1): 1–27.

   2019. *Why Liberalism Works: How True Liberal Values Produce a Freer, More Equal, Prosperous World for All*. New Haven: Yale University Press.

McCloskey, Donald N. 1991. "The Prudent Peasant: New Findings on Open Fields." *Journal of Economic History* 51(2): 343–55.

McGinnis, Michael D. 2005. "Beyond Individualism and Spontaneity: Comments on Peter Boettke and Christopher Coyne." *Journal of Economic Behavior & Organization* 57(2): 167–72.

   2011. "An Introduction to IAD and the Language of the Ostrom Workshop: A Simple Guide to a Complex Framework." *Policy Studies Journal* 39(1): 169–83.

McGuire, Martin C., and Mancur Olson. 1996. "The Economics of Autocracy and Majority Rule: The Invisible Hand and the Use of Force." *Journal of Economic Literature* 34(1): 72–96.

Mehlum, Halvor, Karl Moene, and Ragnar Torvik. 2006. "Institutions and the Resource Curse." *The Economic Journal* 116(508): 1–20.

Menger, Carl. 1892. "On the Origin of Money." *Economic Journal* 2: 239–55.

Menkhaus, Ken. 2007. "Governance without Government in Somalia: Spoilers, State Building, and the Politics of Coping." *International Security* 31(3): 74–106.

Migot-Adholla, Shem E. et al. 1994. "Land, Security of Tenure, and Productivity in Ghana." In *Searching for Land Tenure Security in Africa*, eds. John W. Bruce and Shem E. Migot-Adholla. Dubuque: Kendall/Hunt Publishing Co., 97–118.

Miller, Melinda C. (forthcoming). "'The Righteous and Reasonable Ambition for Forty Acres and a Mule:' Land and Racial Inequality in the Postbellum South." *Review of Economics and Statistics*.

   2011. "Land and Racial Wealth Inequality." *American Economic Review* 101 (3): 371–76.

Mises, Ludwig von. 1935. "Economic Calculation in the Socialist Commonwealth." In *Collectivist Economic Planning*, ed. Friedrich A. Hayek. London: Routledge and Kegan.

Mokyr, Joel. 1990. *The Lever of Riches: Technological Creativity and Economic Progress*. New York: Oxford University Press.

Moore, Barrington. 1966. *Social Origins of Dictatorship and Democracy Lord and Peasant in the Making of the Modern World*. New York: Beacon.

Murtazashvili, Ilia. 2013. *The Political Economy of the American Frontier*. New York: Cambridge University Press.

2017. "Institutions and the Shale Boom." *Journal of Institutional Economics* 13(1): 189–210.

Murtazashvili, Ilia, and Jennifer Murtazashvili. 2015. "Anarchy, Self-Governance, and Legal Titling." *Public Choice* 162(3): 287–305.

2016a. "Can Community-Based Land Adjudication and Registration Improve Household Land Tenure Security? Evidence from Afghanistan." *Land Use Policy* 55: 230–39.

2016b. "Does the Sequence of Land Reform and Political Reform Matter? Evidence from State-Building in Afghanistan." *Conflict, Security & Development* 16(2): 145–72.

2016c. "The Origins of Property Rights: States or Customary Organizations?" *Journal of Institutional Economics* 12(1): 105–28.

2016d. "When Does the Emergence of a Stationary Bandit Lead to Property Insecurity?" *Rationality and Society* 28(3): 335–60.

2019. "The Political Economy of Legal Titling." *Review of Austrian Economics* 32: 251–68.

Murtazashvili, Jennifer. 2016. *Informal Order and the State in Afghanistan*. New York: Cambridge University Press.

Murtazashvili, Jennifer Brick, and Ilia Murtazashvili. (forthcoming). *Land, the State, and War: Property Rights and Political Order in Afghanistan*. Cambridge University Press.

Murtazashvili, Jennifer, and Ilia Murtazashvili. 2020. "Wealth-Destroying States." *Public Choice* 182(3–4): 353–71.

Myerson, Roger. 2004. "Justice, Institutions, and Multiple Equilibria." *Chicago Journal of International Law* 5: 91.

North, Douglass C. 1981. *Structure and Change in Economic History*. New York: W. W. Norton & Company.

1990. *Institutions, Institutional Change and Economic Performance*. New York: Cambridge University Press.

2005. *Understanding the Process of Economic Change*. Princeton: Princeton University Press.

North, Douglass C., and Andrew Rutten. 1987. "The Northwest Ordinance in Historical Perspective." *Essays on the Economy of the Old Northwest*: 19–31.

North, Douglass C., and Robert Paul Thomas. 1973. *The Rise of the Western World: A New Economic History.* New York: Cambridge University Press.

North, Douglass C., John Joseph Wallis, and Barry R. Weingast. 2009. *Violence and Social Orders: A Conceptual Framework for Interpreting Recorded Human History.* New York: Cambridge University Press.

North, Douglass C., and Barry R. Weingast. 1989. "Constitutions and Commitment: The Evolution of Institutions Governing Public Choice in Seventeenth-Century England." *Journal of Economic History* 49(4): 803–32.

Nugent, Jeffrey B., and Nicolas Sanchez. 1993. "Tribes, Chiefs, and Transhumance: A Comparative Institutional Analysis." *Economic Development and Cultural Change* 42(1): 87–113.

Nunn, Nathan. 2008. "The Long-Term Effects of Africa's Slave Trades." *The Quarterly Journal of Economics* 123(1): 139–76.

Oi, Jean C. 1999. *Rural China Takes Off: Institutional Foundations of Economic Reform.* University of California Press.

Olson, Mancur. 1993. "Dictatorship, Democracy, and Development." *American Political Science Review* 87(3): 567–76.

  2000. *Power and Prosperity: Outgrowing Communist and Capitalist Dictatorships.* New York: Basic Books.

Ostrom, Elinor. 1990. *Governing the Commons: The Evolution of Institutions for Collective Action.* New York: Cambridge University Press.

  1999. "Revisiting the Commons: Local Lessons, Global Challenges." *Science* 284(5412): 278–82.

  2007. "A Diagnostic Approach for Going beyond Panaceas." *Proceedings of the National Academy of Sciences* 104(39): 15181–87.

  2009. "A General Framework for Analyzing Sustainability of Social-Ecological Systems." *Science* 325(5939): 419–22.

  2010a. "Beyond Markets and States: Polycentric Governance of Complex Economic Systems." *American Economic Review* 100(3): 641–72.

  2010b. "Polycentric Systems for Coping with Collective Action and Global Environmental Change." *Global environmental change* 20(4): 550–57.

Ostrom, Elinor, and Toh-Kyeong Ahn. 2009. "The Meaning of Social Capital and Its Link to Collective Action." In *Handbook of Social Capital: The Troika of Sociology, Political Science and Economics*, eds. Gert Tinggaard Svendsen and Gunnar Lind Haase Svendsen. Cheltenham: Edward Elgar, 17–35.

Ostrom, Elinor, Marco A. Janssen, and John M. Anderies. 2007. "Going beyond Panaceas." *Proceedings of the National Academy of Sciences* 104(39): 15176–78.

Ostrom, Vincent. 2008. *The Political Theory of a Compound Republic: Designing the American Experiment.* Lanham, MD: Lexington Books.

Ostrom, Vincent, Charles M. Tiebout, and Robert Warren. 1961. "The Organization of Government in Metropolitan Areas: A Theoretical Inquiry." *American Political Science Review* 55(4): 831–42.

Palagashvili, Liya, Ennio Piano, and David Skarbek. 2017. *The Decline and Rise of Institutions – A Modern Survey of the Austrian Contribution to the Economic Analysis of Institutions*. New York: Cambridge University Press.

Pennington, Mark. 2013. "Elinor Ostrom and the Robust Political Economy of Common-Pool Resources." *Journal of Institutional Economics* 9(4): 449–68.

Percy, Sarah, and Anja Shortland. 2013. "The Business of Piracy in Somalia." *Journal of Strategic Studies* 36(4): 541–78.

Platteau, Jean-Philippe. 2000. *Institutions, Social Norms and Economic Development*. New York: Routledge.

Posner, Eric A., and E. Glen Weyl. 2017. "Property Is Only Another Name for Monopoly." *Journal of Legal Analysis* 9(1): 51–123.

  2018. *Radical Markets: Uprooting Capitalism and Democracy for a Just Society*. Princeton: Princeton University Press.

Potts, Jason. 2018. "Governing the Innovation Commons." *Journal of Institutional Economics* 14(6): 1025–47.

  2019. *Innovation Commons*. New York: Oxford University Press.

Powell, Benjamin, Ryan Ford, and Alex Nowrasteh. 2008. "Somalia after State Collapse: Chaos or Improvement?" *Journal of Economic Behavior & Organization* 67(3–4): 657–70.

Putnam, Robert D. 1993. "The Prosperous Community." *The American Prospect* 4(13): 35–42.

Putnam, Robert D., Robert Leonardi, and Raffaella Y. Nanetti. 1994. *Making Democracy Work: Civic Traditions in Modern Italy*. Princeton: Princeton University Press.

Qian, Yingyi, and Barry R. Weingast. 1997. "Federalism as a Commitment to Reserving Market Incentives." *Journal of Economic Perspectives* 11(4): 83–92.

Rajan, Raghuram. 2004. "Assume Anarchy." *Finance and Development* 41(3): 56–57.

Riker, William H., and David L. Weimer. 1993. "The Economic and Political Liberalization of Socialism: The Fundamental Problem of Property Rights." *Social Philosophy and Policy* 10(02): 79–102.

  1995. "The Political Economy of Transformation: Liberalization and Property Rights." In *Modern Political Economy: Old Topics, New Directions*. New York: Cambridge University Press, 80–107.

Rithmire, Meg Elizabeth. 2015. *Land Bargains and Chinese Capitalism: The Politics of Property Rights under Reform*. New York: Cambridge University Press.

Rodrik, Dani, Arvind Subramanian, and Francesco Trebbi. 2004. "Institutions Rule: The Primacy of Institutions over Geography and Integration in Economic Development." *Journal of Economic Growth* 9(2): 131–65.

Root, Hilton L. 1989. "Tying the King's Hands – Credible Commitments and Royal Fiscal Policy during the Old Regime." *Rationality and Society* 1(2): 240–58.

Rutten, M. M. 1992. *Selling Wealth to Buy Poverty: The Process of the Individualization of Landownership among the Maasai Pastoralists of Kajiado District, Kenya, 1890–1990*. Saarbrücken, Germany: Verlag breitenbach Publishers.

Safner, Ryan. 2016. "Institutional Entrepreneurship, Wikipedia, and the Opportunity of the Commons." *Journal of Institutional Economics* 12(4): 743–71.

Salter, Alexander William. 2015. "Rights to the Realm: Reconsidering Western Political Development." *American Political Science Review* 109(4): 725–34.

Salter, Alexander William, and Peter T. Leeson. 2014. "Celestial Anarchy." *Cato Journal* 34(3).

Sargeson, Sally. 2012. "Villains, Victims and Aspiring Proprietors: Framing 'Land-Losing Villagers' in China's Strategies of Accumulation." *Journal of Contemporary China* 21(77): 757–77.

2013. "Violence as Development: Land Expropriation and China's Urbanization." *The Journal of Peasant Studies* 40(6): 1063–85.

Schlager, Edella, and Elinor Ostrom. 1992. "Property-Rights Regimes and Natural Resources: A Conceptual Analysis." *Land Economics*: 249–62.

Scott, James C. 1999. *Seeing like a State: How Certain Schemes to Improve the Human Condition Have Failed*. New Haven: Yale University Press.

2009. *The Art of Not Being Governed: An Anarchist History of Upland Southeast Asia*. New Haven: Yale University Press.

Sened, Itai. 1997. *The Political Institution of Private Property*. New York: Cambridge University Press.

Seth, Michael J. 2019. *A Concise History of Korea: From Antiquity to the Present*. Rowman & Littlefield Publishers.

Shinn, Charles Howard. 1884. *Mining Camps: A Study in American Frontier Government*. Charles Scribner's Sons.

Shortland, Anja. 2019. *Kidnap: Inside the Ransom Business*. New York: Oxford University Press.

Shortland, Anja, and Federico Varese. 2016. "State-Building, Informal Governance and Organised Crime: The Case of Somali Piracy." *Political Studies* 64(4): 811–31.

Sjaastad, Espen, and Daniel W. Bromley. 1997. "Indigenous Land Rights in Sub-Saharan Africa: Appropriation, Security and Investment Demand." *World Development* 25(4): 549–62.

    2000. "The Prejudices of Property Rights: On Individualism, Specificity, and Security in Property Regimes." *Development Policy Review* 18(4): 365–89.

Skaperdas, Stergios. 1992. "Cooperation, Conflict, and Power in the Absence of Property Rights." *The American Economic Review*: 720–39.

Skarbek, David. 2011. "Governance and Prison Gangs." *American Political Science Review* 105(04): 702–16.

    2014. *The Social Order of the Underworld: How Prison Gangs Govern the American Penal System*. New York: Oxford University Press.

    2016. "Covenants without the Sword? Comparing Prison Self-Governance Globally." *American Political Science Review* 110(4): 845–62.

    2020. *The Puzzle of Prison Order: Why Life Behind Bars Varies Around the World*. Oxford University Press.

Smith, Adam C., David B. Skarbek, and Bart J. Wilson. 2012. "Anarchy, Groups, and Conflict: An Experiment on the Emergence of Protective Associations." *Social Choice and Welfare* 38(2): 325–53.

Smith, Vernon L., and Bart J. Wilson. 2019. *Humanomics: Moral Sentiments and the Wealth of Nations for the Twenty-First Century*. New York: Cambridge University Press.

Sokoloff, Kenneth L., and Stanley L. Engerman. 2000. "History Lessons: Institutions, Factors Endowments, and Paths of Development in the New World." *Journal of Economic Perspectives* 14(3): 217–32.

de Soto, Hernando. 2000. *The Mystery of Capital: Why Capitalism Triumphs in the West and Fails Everywhere Else*. New York: Basic Books.

    2002. *The Other Path: The Economic Answer to Terrorism*. New York: Basic Books.

Stasavage, David. 2003. *Public Debt and the Birth of the Democratic State: France and Great Britain 1688–1789*. New York: Cambridge University Press.

    2011. *States of Credit: Size, Power, and the Development of European Polities*. Princeton: Princeton University Press.

2014. "Was Weber Right? City Autonomy, Political Oligarchy, and the Rise of Europe." *American Political Science Review* 108(2): 337–354.

Stavins, Robert N. 2011. "The Problem of the Commons: Still Unsettled after 100 Years." *American Economic Review* 101(1): 81–108.

Steele, Abbey. 2011. "Electing Displacement: Political Cleansing in Apartadó, Colombia." *Journal of Conflict Resolution* 55(3): 423–45.

Stern, David I. 2004. "The Rise and Fall of the Environmental Kuznets Curve." *World Development* 32(8): 1419–39.

Storr, Virgil Henry, and Arielle John. 2020. *Cultural Considerations within Austrian Economics*. Cambridge University Press.

Sugden, Robert. 1989. "Spontaneous Order." *Journal of Economic Perspectives* 3(4): 85–97.

Sun, Li, and Peter Ho. 2018. "Formalizing Informal Homes, a Bad Idea: The Credibility Thesis Applied to China's 'Extra-Legal' Housing." *Land Use Policy* 79: 891–901.

Tang, Shipping. 2011. *A General Theory of Institutional Change*. London: Routledge.

Thompson, Earl A. 1974. "Taxation and National Defense." *Journal of Political Economy* 82(4): 755–82.

Thompson, Neil, and Douglas Hanley. 2018. "Science Is Shaped by Wikipedia: Evidence from a Randomized Control Trial." MIT Sloan Research Paper No. 5238–17.

Tiebout, Charles M. 1956. "A Pure Theory of Local Expenditures." *Journal of Political Economy* 64(5): 416–24.

Tilly, Charles. 1990. *Coercion Capital and European States: AD 990–1990*. Oxford: Blackwell.

Tripp, Aili Mari. 1997. *Changing the Rules: The Politics of Liberalization and the Urban Informal Economy in Tanzania*. Berkeley: University of California Press.

2004. "Women's Movements, Customary Law, and Land Rights in Africa: The Case of Uganda." *African Studies Quarterly* 7(4): 1–19.

Troesken, Werner. 2015. *The Pox of Liberty: How the Constitution Left Americans Rich, Free, and Prone to Infection*. Chicago, IL: University of Chicago Press.

Tsai, Kellee S. 2007. *Capitalism without Democracy: The Private Sector in Contemporary China*. Cornell University Press.

Tullock, Gordon. 1967. "The Welfare Costs of Tariffs, Monopolies, and Theft." *Economic Inquiry* 5(3): 224–32.

Tyler, Tom R. 2006. "Psychological Perspectives on Legitimacy and Legitimation." *Annual Review of Psychology* 57: 375–400.

Umbeck, John. 1977. "A Theory of Contract Choice and the California Gold Rush." *Journal of Law and Economics* 20: 421.

1981. *A Theory of Property Rights: With Application to the California Gold Rush*. Ames: Iowa State University Press.

Vahabi, Mehrdad. 2004. *The Political Economy of Destructive Power*. Cheltenham: Edward Elgar Publishing.

2011. "Appropriation, Violent Enforcement, and Transaction Costs: A Critical Survey." *Public Choice* 147(1–2): 227–53.

2015. *The Political Economy of Predation: Manhunting and the Economics of Escape*. New York: Cambridge University Press.

2016. "A Positive Theory of the Predatory State." *Public Choice* 168(3–4): 153–75.

2020. "Introduction: A Symposium on the Predatory State." *Public Choice* 182: 233–242.

Wagner, Richard E. 2016. *Politics as a Peculiar Business: Insights from a Theory of Entangled Political Economy*. Cheltenham: Edward Elgar Publishing.

Weimer, David L. 1997. "The Political Economy of Property Rights." In *The Political Economy of Property Rights: Institutional Change and Credibility in the Reform of Centrally Planned Economies*, ed. David L. Weimer. New York: Cambridge University Press.

Weingast, Barry R. 1995. "The Economic Role of Political Institutions: Market-Preserving Federalism and Economic Development." *Journal of Law, Economics, and Organization* 11(1): 1–31.

1997. "The Political Foundations of Democracy and the Rule of Law." *American Political Science Review* 91(2): 245–63.

2017. "Adam Smith's Theory of Violence and the Political Economics of Development." In *Organizations*, Civil Society, and the Roots of Development, eds. Naomi R. Lamoreaux and John Joseph Wallis. Chicago: University of Chicago Press, 51–81.

Wiggins, Steven N., and Gary D. Libecap. 1985. "Oil Field Unitization: Contractual Failure in the Presence of Imperfect Information." *American Economic Review* 75(3): 368–85.

Williamson, Claudia R. 2009. "Informal Institutions Rule: Institutional Arrangements and Economic Performance." *Public Choice* 139(3–4): 371–87.

Williamson, Claudia R., and Carrie B. Kerekes. 2011. "Securing Private Property: Formal versus Informal Institutions." *Journal of Law and Economics* 54(3): 537–72.

Wintrobe, Ronald. 2018. "Il Padrino's Dilemma: A Simple Model of Mafia Decision Making." *Journal of Public Finance and Public Choice* 33(1): 45–61.

Wittfogel, Karl. 1957. *Oriental Despotism: A Comparative Study of Total Power.* New Haven: Yale University Press.

Worm, Boris, et al. 2009. "Rebuilding Global Fisheries." *Science* 325(5940): 578–85.

Xu, Chenggang. 2011. "The Fundamental Institutions of China's Reforms and Development." *Journal of Economic Literature* 49(4): 1076–1151.

Yandle, Bruce, and Andrew P. Morriss. 2001. "The Technologies of Property Rights: Choice among Alternative Solutions to Tragedies of the Commons." *Ecology Law Quarterly* 28: 123–68.

Young, Andrew T. 2016. "What Does It Take for a Roving Bandit to Settle Down? Theory and an Illustrative History of the Visigoths." *Public Choice* 168(1–2): 75–102.

    2018. "Hospitalitas: Barbarian Settlements and Constitutional Foundations of Medieval Europe." *Journal of Institutional Economics* 14(4): 715–37.

Acknowledgements

Peter Boettke worked with us on the book from its conceptualization to completion and provided exceptional editorial advice on how to improve the quality of the presentation. Many thanks to Annie Toynbee, Aloysius Thomas, and the production team at Cambridge University Press. Peter T. Leeson and Christopher Coyne deserve special thanks for shaping our understanding of property rights. Harry David provided expert copy-editing services and a careful read of the book. We thank the anonymous readers for a careful read and clear guidance for how to improve the manuscript. Financial support for this research from the Center for Governance and Markets at the University of Pittsburgh is gratefully acknowledged.

Cambridge Elements ☰

Austrian Economics

Peter Boettke
George Mason University

Peter Boettke is a Professor of Economics & Philosophy at George Mason University, the BB&T Professor for the Study of Capitalism, and the director of the F. A. Hayek Program for Advanced Study in Philosophy, Politics and Economics at the Mercatus Center at George Mason University.

About the series

This series will primarily be focused on contemporary developments in the Austrian School of Economics and its relevance to the methodological and analytical debates at the frontier of social science and humanities research, and the continuing relevance of the Austrian School of Economics for the practical affairs of public policy throughout the world.

Cambridge Elements ☰

Austrian Economics

Elements in the series